MEANT FOR MORE

Uncover Repressed Trauma to Find Your *Fuego* Within

ELBA RAQUEL

Meant for More
Elba Raquel

Published by
HOPE Publishing House
4756 Crawford Gulch Road
Golden, CO 80403
www.HopePublishingHouse.com
Lisa@LisaJCoaching.com
954.829.5693

Copyright by Elba Raquel Ploum
All Rights Reserved

No part of this book may be reproduced, stored in or introduced into a retrieval system, or transmitted, in any form or by any means (electronic, mechanical, photocopying, recording or otherwise) without the prior written permission of the copyright owner.

ISBN: 979-8-9917381-1-8 (Hardcover)
ISBN: 979-8-9917381-0-1 (eBook)

Manufactured in the United States

10 9 8 7 6 5 4 3 2

Editors: Auriana Renee and Vicki McCown
Book Layout: Opeyemi Ikuborije
Cover Art: Eleonora D.

Praise for *Meant for More*

"Raquel is a determined, sincere, and passionate woman. She once told me she 'has not had an easy life, but a good one.' Read about her fascinating life experiences and how she dealt with them and broke free from depression and repressed trauma in this book, where she offers a path to healing and true freedom."

Dean McCormick, MBA, CPA, Insight Wealth Strategies, LP

"Oh my gosh, get this book now and get copies for your girlfriends! Elba Raquel's adventures are so relatable to what we as women go through—we're trained to quell the fire within us even though we have the capacity to shine! And Raquel shows us the way. We get a close-up look at her life, a huge gift in itself, but more importantly, we get to see how she overcame her challenges to light that fire again. I love that Raquel learned from her life and created a framework to help others. Add *Meant for More* to your book group list and support each other in shining brightly!"

Kelly McGrath, Esq.

"If you are grappling with the effects of abuse and depression, I wholeheartedly recommend *Meant for More*. This book could very well be the first step on your journey to freedom and self-love."

Martha Broussard

"Could not stop reading! I highly recommend this book to anyone who has experienced trauma in their life and is having a difficult time overcoming it."

Ashley Holland

"*Meant for More* is heartbreaking and uplifting all at the same time. Anyone looking for a method to keep your mindset up and your anxiety down should read this! Truly empowering—it shows you that you can overcome anything!"

Jenna Urmstron

"*Meant for More* is a true gift for anyone on a journey of healing. Raquel's four-step formula is transformative, offering a compassionate guide to overcoming suppressed trauma. Her stories and insights are powerful. I highly recommend this book for those ready to reclaim their peace and inner strength."

Kelly Lorene, Author of *It's a Lifestyle Thing*

"A powerful story of survival, resilience, family, and love. A must-read for everyone, especially those navigating unresolved trauma."

Julie Green, Author of *A Thousand Little Memories*

Acknowledgements

I feel beyond blessed to be able to make something that I talked about doing for a number of years, that I had long considered a dream, into the reality that is *Meant for More*. I am thankful and grateful to have so many supportive people. I would like to give a special thanks to:

Elba Hortencia - My beautiful, classy, elegant, graceful, intelligent firecracker that was my mother. I am my mother's daughter—I get my *fuego* from you. Words do not exist to describe how much I miss you. I continue to be in awe of you and inspired by you. I love you more than words can ever say.

Ashley Holland - My gorgeous daughter, inside and out. From the moment you were born, you have brought a tremendous amount of love, laughter, sass, and so much fun and joy into my life! You put the sparkle into my life. I admire your continued undying determination to be your authentic self with such grace and style. I'm not kidding when I say I want to be just like you when I grow up! I am beyond blessed and proud to be your Momma-Dukes.

Elijah Smith - My McGoo! My handsome son. You are such a blessing in my life! You say I am your life coach, but *you* have taught *me* so much about life. You have taught me patience (phew!), the true meaning of unconditional love, and the ability to find something positive in any situation. You are a good man with a kind soul. Continue to live in your own authenticity. I am grateful and honored to be your mom.

Mia Marie Holland - My beautiful, stunning, gorgeous granddaughter. I love you. I love you. I love you. You have brought so much joy and love into my life! You have given me a sense of purpose that I have never felt before. I look forward to many more Mia and Mina days filled with laughter, cuddles, neverending kisses and hugs—not to mention our many conversations about anything and everything. Mia and Mina dance parties are absolutely the best!

Steve Holland - I won the son-in-law lottery with you! Thank you for being you and for loving our girls the way that you do. It is heartwarming to witness in the everyday minutia. Your kindness, thoughtfulness, and considerate heart shines through in Mia. She is the best of you and Ashley, all wrapped into one gorgeous being! World, look out!

Martha Broussard - Your sisterly phone calls and conversations have been a bright light in the process of writing this book. Thank you for your continued support, love, and laughter. It is all love and always appreciated! I love you, sis.

Lisa Jimenez - Where do I begin? Without you in my life I would not have written *Meant for More*. You, your coaching, your Mindset Retreats, Hope Publishing House's Author's Coaching Program, and *especially* your friendship have changed my life! Thank you for being you and for all that you do. I love you, my friend.

Auriana Renee - My dear friend. Thank you for making the writing process so much easier. You have a wonderful way of getting me to put my thoughts and emotions on paper. I have often been surprised at how well you knew me. Your knowledge and expertise is greatly appreciated! You are one of my favorite people. I love you, Auri!

Vicki McCown - This book has more depth because of your editing, thought-provoking questions, and expertise. Thank you. I am forever grateful.

My Vienna Ladies - You all know who you are! I adore each and everyone of you. Thank you for continuing to be a positive and supportive force in my life. Forever grateful to each of you for your friendships. Let's continue creating new experiences and memories together. I love you all!

My Bali Babes - All of you brought such positive energy into my life at a time when I needed it the most. It was so reinvigorating. And I am forever grateful. Thank you for making Bali even more special. Bali has been special to me not just because of the beauty, but because of the magical time we all shared there.

I look forward to making more memories with each of you. I love you all!

My Fellow Authors:

Kelly Cummings - You have continued to surprise me every step of the way of our writing journey. I have seen you grow stronger, more confident and serene right before my eyes. I am beyond happy and excited for you to experience all that is to come with your book. Let's continue having fun on this wonderful journey we are on!

Julie Green - Crossing the finish line of this incredible writing journey while walking alongside you is truly one of my 'something better's. From the moment we met, you have continually impressed me. The more I get to know you, the more you inspire me. Let's continue having fun creating memories like the ones from the Shönbrunn Zoo in Vienna, Austria—what a day!

Tiffany Hibbard - Thank you for being you. You made me think, woman! Your kind words have always meant the world to me. I love and appreciate you!

Dedication

It is with all my heart and soul that I dedicate this book to my amazing, awe-inspiring children, Ashley and Elijah. Thank you from the bottom of my heart for always being your authentic selves. Because of you I continue to strive to be a better me! I love you through the stars, around the moon…and back.

   I love you more.

CONTENTS

Praise for *Meant for More*. i

Acknowledgements. v

Dedication ix

Introduction: Oh, It's You! 1

Letter to Me from Self-Love 6

Chapter 1: Façade 9

Chapter 2: Abused 19

Chapter 3: Black Baby Doll 33

Chapter 4: Not My Mistake to Make 45

Chapter 5: White Knight in Shining Armor 51

Chapter 6: South African Delights. 67

Chapter 7: Utsukushii—Profoundly Beautiful 81

Chapter 8: Paris...the City of Love? 97

Chapter 9: I Am My Mother's Daughter. 103

Chapter 10: Space and Grace. 119

Letter to My Reader from Me *132*

Chapter 11: In God I Trust 135

Chapter 12: A New Legacy. 143

Chapter 13: Mia Is a Happy Girl! 153

Letter to Depression from Me *161*

Epilogue. 163

My Notes 167

INTRODUCTION

Oh, It's You!

Terrified by how tiny I was, my mom carried me around the house on a tiny pillow. She was afraid she would drop me without it. She didn't know what else to do—there was no NICU in 1965, no book on how to care for a four-pound, three-ounce preemie. I was a little bitty thing, more skin than anything else, lying on my stomach with my knees bent and my tiny butt propped up in the air. I looked like a large, brown frog. Literally the size of a frog. Can you imagine? And because of that, I was treated delicately.

I've always been small for my age. Even as an adult, I'm very petite, but I am far from delicate. I survived that too-small infant body through pure tenacity. What my mom didn't realize at the time was that her preemie baby was already full of *fuego*—a fierce fire and passion for life. My body may have been small, but my spirit, my *fuego*, has always burned larger than life. It's that inner flame that has pushed me through every challenge and shaped the person I am today.

Even so, I have had my moments of spiritual smallness. Throughout my life, I often allowed other people and this tough world to silence my voice and suppress my shining spirit.

I have experienced abusive relationships, harmful family dynamics, and the horrible effects of racism and classism. I have lived with depression—a condition that ran in my family and was definitely exacerbated by the hardships I had to face. This led to my becoming listless, drifting through life in survival mode, just taking care of my kids and focusing on getting from moment to moment.

For a while I thought I had escaped my depression by marrying a stable and supportive man who took me across the world from my problems. But even in that phase of security and ease, I still found myself unfulfilled. My tenacious spirit, that *fuego* within me, was so stifled that I could barely hear it anymore. All I knew was that its tiny voice inside kept whispering that I was meant for more.

Do you hear it too? That whisper that you are meant for more? So many of us hear that call and have no idea how to answer. We feel lost, hurt, and utterly alone—trapped in lives that do not fill our souls. We're sad and tired and frustrated at the world for tearing us down. We crave that sense of purpose, that zeal for life, that *fuego* within but do not know where to find it.

We seek validation from our families, our friends, our lovers, and the world itself. And the sad truth? They will always disappoint. No one can give us all the love we need. This leads to depression, loneliness, and a lack of purpose. We get lost in the numbness and forget who the hell we are!

I learned the hard way that we will never find our value or authentic joy in any status, experience, or person. My life went from the lowest low to a fairytale dream, and I still could not muster any of the passion for life I craved. The loving husband didn't fix me. Neither did the money or the travel. It was not until I searched within that I reawakened my authenticity and accessed the "more" I had always sought. It was in me all along.

In this book, I share my life story: How I lifted myself out of depression and found the "more" I was meant for within myself. How I remembered who I really am, who I was meant to be. I will teach you my proven EIF—Emotional Intelligence Formula—for accessing your authenticity, honed through a lifetime of personal experience, so you too can live the life you were meant for. Everything you have been looking for is right there within you, and my stories and lessons will show you how to tap into it. There is no need to seek it anywhere else or from anyone else.

This book is also a love letter to my children, so they can understand their mother and know that depression is not their only inheritance. Joy is also a family legacy. Living full-out in their authentic uniqueness is their birthright.

My kids know one of the little things that has always helped me feel my *fuego* is shoes. I am a sucker for a killer pair of shoes, especially heels. I am no Imelda Marcos, but I have some really lovely heels: stilettos, platforms, kittens, mules, slingbacks, wedges. Oh, and of course, Mary Janes. My first pair of special shoes were Mary Janes.

I was five years old when my mom bought them for me. I was in love! I loved the one-inch heel, the extra shiny, black-patent leather, and most of all, the clickety-clack they made when I walked. Even at five, they made me feel feminine. I felt like a woman. Shoes were a big deal in my family—my mom and her fellow Latina friends all wore heels, and they would NEVER go out in cheap or casual shoes.

One day, while my mom and her friends were gathered in the kitchen sharing Bundt cake, coffee, and gossip, I walked from the front of the house to join them. We lived in a New Orleans shotgun house, so there was a long unbroken hallway from the front door to the kitchen in the back. My Mary Janes clickety-clacked along the hardwood floor the whole way. And let me tell you, I was feeling myself. I swayed my hips like my mom down the hallway and pretended it was a runway. When I entered the kitchen, my mom looked up in surprise. She laughed and said, "Oh, it's you!"

I walked with so much sass, she thought another of her friends had arrived in her grown-up heels. Instead, her tiny five year old, once a baby so small and delicate she had to be carried on a pillow, strutted into the room. I will never forget that exclamation. "Oh, it's you!" In that moment, she saw *me* for the first time. Her confident, sassy, feisty, beautiful daughter. Full of Latina *fuego* and not so delicate after all.

That feisty little girl was lost for years, but I finally found her again. And you can, too. No matter what the world has thrown at you, you have that spirit within you. You can find that *fuego* inside you. If you are willing to follow my formula, take accountability for your life, and stay open, vulnerable, and honest, I promise you will find your own empowered authenticity, and in it an unbridled excitement for life. You will not only like yourself, you will fall in love with yourself. That small voice inside you is right—you *are* meant for more: more love, more joy, more depth, more self-worth. I ask you… What greater gift is there to give yourself?

You are not alone. I was right where you are—depressed and isolated with no clue where to go from here. And, if I can find my way back to my *fuego*…

So. Can. You.

Letter to Me from Self-Love

Dear Elbita,

I hope you don't mind me calling you by your childhood nickname—Elbita. You've softened through your healing journey, and it reminds me of who you were as a child. That name suits you perfectly—endearing, joyful, and always striving to be your best self. Though petite in size, you've always had a fierce spirit. What you lack in height, you make up for with fuego: love, strength, feistiness, power, courage, and determination. You came into this world so tiny, yet so fiercely tenacious. That same strength and courage have pulled you out of the dark and into the light. You've done the hard work, for yourself and by yourself. You invested your energy and love into your own growth, understanding that without the dark, the light wouldn't shine so brightly. I applaud you for that.

Keep giving yourself grace on this journey of self-expansion and emotional intelligence as you become the best version of yourself. I am so proud of everything you've accomplished—and I hope you are too! It's been an incredible amount of inner work to reach the goals you set for yourself, and you did it. I see you, I appreciate you, and I celebrate you.

Take a moment to pat yourself on the back and acknowledge all the hard work it took to get where you are today. It wasn't easy—it was one of the hardest things you've ever done. But here you are, stronger and more self-aware than ever.

Continue this beautiful journey of self-healing. Give yourself space, grace, and self-love—especially for the changes only you know about. You are truly the only person that matters in your own self-approval. If you love who you are today, everyone who is meant to be in your life will show up, in perfect timing, to love you for exactly who you are.

I see you. I honor you. I love you.

Forever grateful,
Self-Love

CHAPTER 1

Façade

One day in the fourth grade, I asked to go home from school early. I distinctly remember having a bad head cold. My sister Elizabeth came to pick me up. She had walked to the school, which meant we had to trek the ten blocks home. I carried my school bag all the way.

Backpacks weren't as popular in the seventies, or at least I didn't have one, so I carried a thick two-handled plastic book bag over one shoulder. It was heavy, full of books, notebooks, and other supplies. I was sick, and between feeling weak and carrying the heavy bag, I couldn't keep pace with Elizabeth. I gave up trying, and she was a good block ahead of me most of the walk. She turned around once to check that I was still behind her and rolled her eyes at my slow pace.

When we were less than a block away from our home, our mother drove by on the way home from errands. Suddenly, Elizabeth perked up. She walked back to me, took my book bag, and carried it for the last half block. When we walked into the house, she made sure she was carrying that bag, heaving a big sigh when putting it down to show how heavy it was. My mom praised her for taking *such* good care of me and being *such* a good big sister. Elizabeth wore a huge, satisfied smile at that praise.

The story of that walk is one small anecdote in what has turned out to be a rather extraordinary life, but I feel compelled to start here. That tired walk is where my angst began.

Don't worry, we'll get to the good stuff. I am full of stories, bursting with them. As I write this, memories surface and more stories appear, waiting to be cataloged and shared. They seem infinite. As you read my stories, you will see my days under Japan's blossoming cherry trees, my nights gathered around the family table for food and card games in Honduras, my desperate escape by train from an abusive husband, my seven-year-old son's suicide note. I share dramatic epics, hilarious slices of life, steamy romances, heart-wrenching sorrows, and sweeping depictions of beauty around the world.

But this story, this arguably mundane story of a small childhood slight, is where we begin. Because for me, it all begins and ends with authenticity. If this is the tale of how that little girl in Mary Janes lost and found herself again, then it has to start with her spirited desire to be herself, and why she feels this is such a radical act.

I learned that day that not everyone is as they seem, and I didn't like the hypocrisy. Other people seemed to be fine with inauthenticity…but not me. I couldn't accept a façade. I didn't like the way it made me feel.

But that feeling of angst did instill in me a strong value of authenticity. Even at nine years old I was aware of the level of integrity that I wanted to live my life by. So much so that being my true self is now the main thread of how I live my life. Living authentically is the greatest joy—it has reignited the *fuego* within me.

Throughout my adult life I have managed depression and anxiety. I would find myself feeling restless, unable to be at ease, uncomfortable in my own skin. No matter where I turned for confirmation that I would be okay, I never found it. I was on prescribed antidepressant and sleeping medication for over fifteen years.

Something in me knew that the life I had was not the one I was meant for. I was meant for more.

During Covid, I experienced true solitude, and being with myself forced me to confront the truth: I was not happy with who I had become, and I was the common denominator in all my worst experiences. Looking outside of myself for validation had led me to live according to other people's expectations, trying to be the person they perceived me as or wanted me to be. I was rounding my edges to fit into others' worlds, ignoring the feisty girl that was the true core of my soul. It's easy to get lost in that, to forget who you are. And I did.

Admitting my part in my depression was a tough pill to swallow. Like Elizabeth's big book-bag smile, my life—my very identity—was a façade. And like the nine-year-old me who felt so betrayed by the lie, I couldn't bear it. *Of course* I was anxious. What a conflict to hold in my soul.

In Chapter 11, I will share how I waded through my darkest shadows to rediscover my authenticity. That's right, no story is off limits here. I bare it all.

In finding what worked for me, I developed a process for rediscovering my *fuego*. I kept doing the same four steps, and they worked. This process helped me to stop my anxiety spirals and feel the untamed joy of life again.

So, I organized this process into a formula to help you do the same. I share it here in the hope you spot the bones of it in all the high points of my life, and notice the absence of these practices in the low. I also hope you will follow its four steps to find your own *fuego* within you.

Emotional Intelligence Formula:

Step 1 – *Desire to Change*

The first step was giving myself over to the desire to change and to live a more authentic life. A life that represented me, not what people thought of me or even who they wanted me to be. I had to want to live my authentic life by improving myself and my lifestyle with unyielding determination.

Step 2 – *Identify Triggers*

The second step was identifying my triggers; I had to pay attention to what was sparking my panic attacks. Of course, this meant allowing myself to feel all of the uncomfortable feelings that come with them: depression, anxiety, that feeling I sometimes had of not being comfortable in my own skin. That was the hardest part. But over time, I started to notice the same few triggers setting me off. This step also helped me with organizing what I could control in my life and what I couldn't and recognizing that some triggers were completely avoidable.

Sit with the raw emotion of anxiety and ask yourself, "Why? Why am I feeling this?" Identify when you're triggered, and instead of avoiding or suppressing it, sit with those uncomfortable emotions—whether it's anxiety, depression, or PTSD. For example, let's say you're triggered by a certain place that reminds you of a painful memory. When you visit that place, notice the tightness in your chest, the flood of emotion that rises, and instead of pushing it away, let yourself fully feel it.

As you sit with those emotions, ride the wave all the way to the end. If you feel pain, confusion, anger, or frustration, allow yourself to experience every bit of it. Don't rush the process—cry if you need to, express your frustration, but let those emotions flow.

For instance, maybe being in that place brings up feelings of abandonment or betrayal. Acknowledge them—feel them fully. As you ride that emotional wave, you're taking back your power from the trigger. You may feel exhausted afterward, but in that exhaustion is the beginning of your healing.

Each time you do this, you reclaim a piece of your emotional power from that trigger. The more you sit with your emotions and allow yourself to feel, the more you heal. It's uncomfortable, but it's transformative. Slowly, the trigger will hold less power over you, and you will feel a sense of strength and resilience growing from within. That's how the healing process begins—by facing the discomfort head-on, again and again.

Step 3 – *Let. It. Go.*

Step three was to practice letting go of those triggers. For me, visualization helped. I would imagine myself in the driver's seat of a car. Then, I would picture the trigger as an object and put it behind me in the back seat. I couldn't see it anymore unless I looked in the rearview mirror. And I would practice looking forward, resisting the temptation to search for it in the mirror. You will be amazed at how much easier this step gets with consistency and with time. I do not say this lightly. It is the most important step in the entire process. Let. It. Go.

Once you acknowledge the trigger, give yourself space and grace by acknowledging your progress. Some progress only you will be aware of—celebrate the small wins every day by giving grace in knowing, understanding, and admitting times you will need to reach out to family, friends, or therapist for advice, guidance…or just a hug.

Step 4 – *Realign*

Simply realign to the energy of peace and joy by continuing to manage your own energy and emotions. Life will continue to throw you curveballs; in those moments it is a nudge from God simply saying… Nope, that is not where you are meant to be at this point in your life. So, realign back to personal peace and joy.

Bring yourself back to center. Sit in the energy of personal peace, joy, self-love, and self-worth that you have found within yourself by completing my Emotional Intelligence Formula.

To this very day, I continue to repeat this process. Repeat. Repeat. Repeat. I consistently work on who I want to be when I grow up. Please notice I said "who"—not where, not what, but *who* I want to be. I am still exploring the qualities of that person. I continue to try, every day, to be my pure-hearted authentic self.

The first time I intentionally practiced my Emotional Intelligence Formula was the day I had my first acute anxiety attack. I had felt anxious all my adult life, but this was different. I could not sit still. I could not stand still. My heart raced. My hands shook. With each second every feeling intensified, completely taking over every cell of my body. It was getting harder to breathe. I had to tell myself breathe in—breathe out, breathe in—breathe out. I found myself pacing my apartment, walking circles through the living room, the dining room, the kitchen.

Until finally it occurred to me to sit down on my couch. I sat in the anxious energy that was going through my body and allowed myself to sink into the uncomfortableness of it. I took an inventory of everything I was feeling. And I asked myself, "Why?"

Why am I feeling this?

What brought this on?

What was I thinking when it occurred?

What emotions was I feeling when it started?

Once I identified the trigger, I acknowledged it. Then…I let it go.

I repeat, I. Let. It. Go.

Then I realigned. I brought myself back to center. I fostered energy of health, self-love, and self-worth, which my formula has enabled me to find within myself, instead of looking outside.

I breathed an easy breath. In that moment my whole world shifted. I was amazed. The anxiety in my body was gone.

Four months ago, I completely went off my medications, cold turkey. I did not plan to stop them so abruptly, and, if you are on antidepressants, I do not recommend that you do it that way either. It is just how it played out for me. The night before I unexpectedly left my Newport Beach apartment, I took my antidepressant and my sleeping pill for the last time. I was leaving that apartment for my own safety (more on that story later), and I had to have all of my wits about me. It was a full two weeks before I even realized that I had not taken either pill again. Not once. It never occurred to me to take one.

During those weeks, I faced visits from violent stalkers, constant harassment from my sister Elizabeth, and challenges with my family. Yet, I hadn't taken a single pill. I navigated some of the most difficult moments of my life without relying on medication.

I'm sure any physician would say I went about stopping medication the wrong way, and I would not disagree. It's just that by the time I realized I hadn't been on them, I was able to think clearly. I wasn't numb. I did not feel like I was just going through the motions like I had felt so many times before. I rationalized, prioritized, organized, strategized, planned, and executed a cross-country move while going through all of the emotions and exhaustion these circumstances had created in my life. And I did it successfully. Successfully! I am not going to say that it was easy. It wasn't. But! I was not numb through any of it. I felt all the feels, good and bad, that each situation brought on. At the lowest point in my life, I felt alive.

My Emotional Intelligence Formula helped me get there. It is the tool that enabled me to manage my emotions without medication and reconnect with my true self. I hope it does the same for you.

CHAPTER 2

Abused

If you feel triggered when reading this chapter please call:
    24/7 National Domestic Violence Hotline
    Languages: English, Spanish, 200+ through interpretation service
    800-799-7233
    SMS: Text START to 88788

I peeked through the blinds of the front window, heart racing, convinced I would see my husband stride up the sidewalk with a gun in hand. I was so scared I had to remind myself to breathe. I had done this every few minutes for days.

A week before, I told Howard I was leaving. I was taking our two children back to New Orleans to stay with my mother while I figured out how to give them a better life—far from his violent temper. It was a conversation I'll never forget, not just because of what was at stake, but because of Howard's immediate response. Without missing a beat, he looked at me and said,

"What makes you think a man will want you with another man's children?"

We were standing in the kitchen—he was grabbing something from the fridge, and I was preparing dinner. I stopped what I was doing, turned to him, and said, "What makes you think I need a man in my life?" The look of shock on his face was priceless, and I still remember it to this day.

I had been physically, mentally, and emotionally abused for too long. I needed to get out. I didn't say that part out loud, but he knew. I wasn't just leaving Philadelphia—I was leaving him.

We fought about it all night. The next day, he called me from work to tell me that he would kill me with his coworker's gun if I left him. I grabbed the kids and left that instant. I could not pack even one article of clothing. My children and I escaped with just the clothes on our backs.

Delores had arranged for us to stay with a family friend until we could leave town. She made sure to keep it all hidden from Howard. Having witnessed parts of his temper and erratic behavior, she knew how deep his drug habits ran, along with the toxic mindset that came with them. But as the week passed, her tone changed.

One day, she sat down with me, a bit more relaxed, and said, "I think you might be overreacting. Howard's all talk. I don't believe he's actually looking for you, and even if he was, he wouldn't hurt you."

I stopped what I was doing and looked her straight in the eye. "Delores, you don't know what he's capable of," I said, my voice steady but firm. "I'm the only person who does. There's not a soul on this earth who could convince me that he isn't looking for me, or that his intentions aren't dangerous."

She looked surprised, but I continued, "No one's walking in my shoes. No one's feeling what I'm feeling—this fear, stress, rage, guilt, isolation. The weight of the abuse, Delores. No one else sees that like I do."

The silence hung in the air between us, thick with the truth.

The isolation was the worst. We had moved to Philly to be near Howard's family, and they were the only people in town I knew well enough to trust. I had to rely on them for my safety and the safety of my babies. I didn't have anyone else, even just to talk to. Of course Delores softened—Howard was her son. Where were *my* people?

Maybe you also know these feelings all too well. It may feel like it's just you, alone against the world. I get it. But sometimes YOU is all you need. There is so much more within you than you realize right now. You're stronger than you think. I was. We will build on this idea in the next few chapters, but I hope that right now you can just trust and believe. You are not lacking anything, including love and support. You can give those things to yourself. You can be your own support system.

It is here that I have to acknowledge, not just to you but also to myself, that even though I got myself through my abusive marriage, I also could have been who created it. I could have created it by allowing myself to gradually be treated poorly from early on in the relationship. Is that something that you can relate to? I ask—not to place shame or blame on you—but, if so, this could be the opportunity you seek to acknowledge it and to begin to take accountability for it. Do not misunderstand me, it is not your fault. But it is a cycle that only you can break while you still can.

No one knew anything of what I had experienced or what I was feeling in those moments. I had to be my own support system. At the time, that was isolating; but looking back, I see that the reason I made it out was me—and that's empowering. I was not lacking support—everything I needed was right there within me.

I planned our escape carefully. A train to New Orleans made the most sense, but Howard worked across the street from the train station. I couldn't risk him catching us. So, I made arrangements for us to take a bus to Detroit, then a train the rest of the way to New Orleans. My plan worked; Howard did not expect us to take a bus. We made it safely to Detroit. Once we arrived at the train station, I informed security about my situation and Howard's threats. They let me sit in front of the security office where we could be observed at all times. I sat on that bench and held my children in terror. Even with all that distance between us, I still feared Howard would find me. The minutes trickled by until, finally, our train pulled into the station. I don't think I let out a full breath until we made it home.

Thankfully, my mother's house was safe. Howard kept sending threats from Philly, but he never came to New Orleans to find me. Still, it was months before I could be in a crowd without looking over my shoulder. Howard's violence had become a defining feature of my world.

How did I get here? How did that feisty little girl who could strut down the hall like a grown Latina turn into this scared woman, letting her life be shaped by someone else's mistakes? A lot had happened in between. Somewhere along the way, I stopped listening to that tenacious spirit inside of me. It didn't begin with Howard—it began with me. I stopped listening to the girl in the Mary Janes. I may have extinguished my own *fuego* without even realizing it.

As women, we often prioritize family—holding it together, making sacrifices, doing whatever it takes to keep things running smoothly. And sometimes, without realizing it, we lose ourselves in the process, all for the good of those we love. Looking back, I see that's something I learned from my mother. I watched her try to make it work with my stepfather, doing everything she could to keep the peace. I'll never forget the first time I saw her smack the wall in frustration because he refused to acknowledge her. That moment opened my eyes to the state of their marriage.

Mom did her best to shield us from the worst of it, like so many parents do, hiding the 'adult stuff.' She kept her composure, carrying on as though she had no concerns in the world. So, by the time I realized how bad things really were, I was confused. I could sense there were problems—it had become too obvious to ignore—but her energy with us, her two youngest daughters still at home, stayed steady. She didn't let on how much she was carrying.

Unfortunately, that was learned behavior for me. I leaned into the same patterns with both Howard and Roger, holding onto the belief that if I just kept trying—if my heart was in the right place—the marriage would survive. I convinced myself that all I had to do was keep my head above water while burying it in the sand, avoiding the conflicts to maintain whatever fragile peace remained. Have you ever done that? Had the best intentions but with the wrong focus? It's a confusing, maddening cycle—trying to figure out how to navigate the mess without losing yourself entirely.

I was seventeen when I met Howard at Georgie Porgie's lounge in the Hyatt Regency in downtown New Orleans. Howard told me he was twenty-four, though I found out after we were living together that he was actually twenty-six. I lived at home with my mother and my younger sister, Janeth. I was a typical teenager who enjoyed going out dancing, and somehow I never got carded. Ironically, I started to get carded after I was a young mother of legal age. Go figure! I worked full time and went out dancing every Wednesday through Sunday. There were times I would get home with only enough time to shower, change, and head straight to work.

I was too young to be involved in a relationship with Howard—with any twenty-six-year-old man. But, of course, that thought never occurred to me. I was already living like an adult—so mature, or so I thought. The first night I spent with Howard I stayed over. Then I stayed the next night. And the next. We basically lived together from then on. Howard was a partier, and I loved to go out dancing. I was too young to notice that those two activities were not the same thing. We both stayed out all night, and I, blinded by love, didn't notice the extent of the drugs.

I was nineteen when I got pregnant with Ashley, and Howard promised to settle down and be a good father. Ashley was born in New Orleans Charity Hospital when I was twenty. A year later, we moved to Philadelphia, Howard's home town. That's when we got married.

The day I married Howard, I knew in my gut that it was not going to last. I had seen enough of his partying and his temper to know he was not ready to be a husband or father. But I kept walking down that "aisle." (We got married by the Justice of the Peace in Philadelphia, so there wasn't really an aisle to speak of.) I put one foot in front of the other. Howard was Ashley's father, so I had to give it a try, didn't I? I felt that I owed it to Ashley, the light of my life, to try to keep our little family together. My intuition fought that notion with every step. This would not be good for me. Yet, here I was, putting one foot…in front…of the other. Then I was standing in front of a Justice of the Peace, saying, "I do." I was a young twenty-one-year-old, hoping for the best—going against my intuition and ignoring the feeling in my gut. And of course, that intuition was not wrong. The marriage did not last.

This is the first time I can recall choosing not to listen to my inner self. If only I had listened then, I would have avoided all the pain that came after.

We stayed with Delores until she was able to secure an apartment for us in her building. She lived on the third floor; we lived on the eighth. We had a home, we had support from

Delores, and, best of all, we had a perfect little girl. Still, something in me knew I wasn't safe. My intuition said Howard was angry and unreliable, and it was only a matter of time before our little fairytale crumbled. I had ignored that feeling when I married him, and I continued to ignore it. We had our son, Elijah, almost two years later.

At some point, Howard started going out again. The drugs came back. Eventually he started staying out all night. Then all night turned into several days. When he did eventually make it home, his entire paycheck would be gone. He would yell at me for his feeling trapped, and eventually that anger turned physical. I was physically, mentally, emotionally, and financially abused in that marriage. And I learned that people will do to you what you allow them to do. I should have listened to my intuition.

On one of these occasions, Howard had been missing for several days and came home only to demand that I give him the last bit of cash I had. I had hidden some money in a large glass jar of white rice that I kept on top of the refrigerator. I refused to tell him where it was. He searched the apartment himself, becoming increasingly angry. He shouted at me, cussed me out, punched a hole in the wall. Eventually, he grabbed a knife and chased me around our round glass kitchen table. Yes, you read that right, a knife. We ran in circles, him yelling, me crying. At one point, we stopped in a standoff on opposite sides of the table, and I caught sight of Ashley. She was hiding behind one of the kitchen chairs at the table. Her tiny hands gripped the spindles in fear as she peeked between them. She was three years old.

The terror in her eyes is etched into my brain. In that moment, I saw that ignoring my inner spirit and stifling my voice didn't just hurt me, it hurt my children. I owed it to myself, and especially to my children, to speak up. To step up. This was not the way I wanted to raise them. I wanted Ashley to know she deserved to be treated better than this, and I wanted Elijah to know that it is never okay for any man to treat a woman this way. Most of all, I wanted them safe.

I realized that, even though Howard was eight years older than me, I had outgrown him. I could do a much better job raising our children alone. It was time to leave Philadelphia, Howard, and that painful chapter of my life behind. This time, I made the final decision to leave him—for good. I had left Howard before, and he had made promises before, only to break them again. But something was different this time. Once I admitted to myself that I had outgrown him, I knew I was done with every aspect of that marriage. There was no going back.

I have come to understand that I walked down that aisle and married Howard because I deeply wanted to be wrong. I loved him for the man that he could be, not the man that he actually was. I wanted my forever with him and our little family. I wanted it so badly that I chose to ignore my intuition. Have you ever done that? Don't you sometimes hate it when you are right? I didn't know exactly what would happen, but I knew enough. And I still married him.

It's hard to hold ourselves accountable for our choices when so much of the blame belongs to others. Howard hurt me, and I did not deserve it. But I chose to ignore my intuition, and to shove down my *fuego* in the hope of being wrong. That is something I can own. That was my choice. Learning to listen to my inner voice was my first step toward a better life. I had to learn to trust my intuition, to listen to my gut. I've since honed in on it, and it has not steered me wrong since. We need to learn to understand our bodies and what they're trying to tell us at any given time. To trust that we *do* know what is best for ourselves.

So that is your first step. Sit in silence and listen to yourself.

Close your eyes. While taking long deep breaths, analyze—from top to bottom—how you are feeling in this moment. Pay attention to your emotions. What are you feeling? Anxious, nervous, peaceful? Learn to feel and understand your own energy. What is it saying to you?

For too long I walked through life with so much unrecognized anxiety that it ended up leading to my depression. I have since learned to recognize my own energy, including when I am feeling anxious, so it does not lead to worse feelings. Your inner voice is always trying to tell you something. It is up to you to learn how to listen to it.

So, did you do it? Did you really sit in silence? I know, it is not easy. It takes courage to be so raw and honest because we won't always like what we find out about ourselves. Please do not read on until you give yourself that gift of self-reflection.

Take this time to give yourself the grace, and the space to sit in complete silence.

Let's get back to my story…my intuition ended up being right. I was able to raise my kids on my own. I gave them a better life than Howard and I could have together. I really did it. Even with my apprehension. Even with my fear. Even with the exhaustion of the responsibility weighing heavily on me, I did it.

I really don't know how I pushed aside my fears and apprehensions. I just did. I did what I had to do. Every day. I worked as a restaurant supervisor. Often, I would go weeks without a day off, but that was okay. I was stable. So much so that I could pay my mother weekly to take care of Ashley and Elijah. Delores and/or Howard would send me money to help from time to time, but I was almost always our children's sole provider. Somehow, I was always able to provide everything my kids needed. In a way, it was miraculous. I look back at that time in my life in awe of myself. Sometimes I even wonder where the hell that version of me went! But, she was there for me. She was a force to be reckoned with, and she showed up every time I needed her to. Who knew I had her in me?!

My intuition told me that my life would be better without Howard, and I was right. Imagine how much pain I would have avoided if I'd listened to my gut the first time. Though my life with Howard was a disaster, I would not have my kids without that relationship. I cannot regret it. And I would do it all over again to ensure that I would get my two babies, Ashley and Elijah. They are the best part of my life!

My relationship with Howard was the first of many where I suppressed my intuition and ignored my inner voice. But what did I know? I didn't feel like I knew enough about life or that I had experienced enough of it to understand what was best for me. You know? Have you ever felt so small compared to the world, to life, that you convince yourself that everyone else who's had more experiences must know best? I should have stood up for that feisty little girl inside me. I regret not having more of a backbone. I regret not embracing the *fuego* within me before it began to fade.

What I am saying is that I could have taken more accountability in my life at the time. I made the decision to stay far too long in a relationship that I knew wasn't going to succeed. I put my natural tenacity into clinging to the false hope that Howard would surprise me, leaving no stone unturned as I searched for ways to make our family work. That tenacity can be a good trait to have, but looking back on my life, I see that I turned over too many stones before I admitted to myself that it was time to set boundaries and move on.

Do you have that trait?

Well, don't fret. Learn from my mistakes; learn from my lessons. Take accountability for your choices. Sit with them. Sit with the emotions that they evoke. And if you feel the need to, change. Now is the time to start. But remember it is a process, it will take some time. Be consistent with your intentions and be honest with yourself every step of the way. Consistency is key. And over time, your life will change.

Both *repressed trauma* and *suppressed trauma* are about removing mental content from your awareness. Repression is generally unconscious, and suppression is generally conscious.

I had to educate myself on the difference between repressed and suppressed trauma. Now that I am a little more educated on the difference between the two, I can confidently state that I *repressed* my trauma in my marriage to Howard. I had to. In order to do what I had to do every day to raise my babies, I had to repress it. Until I didn't.

Repressed trauma is when you unconsciously disassociate yourself from trauma. It normally means a person has not dealt with the emotions that come with repressed trauma, e.g., fear, anger.

I didn't heal from my repressed trauma from my marriage to Howard until I started writing *Meant for More*, which brought up these memories, especially those regarding my children. I sat in the emotions they evoked and worked my EIF consistently.

Suppressed trauma is when you consciously choose not to think about your experiences and the pain they cause. It is a choice,

In my second marriage, I *suppressed* my trauma—trauma from those situations that hurt my feelings. From not being heard. From my feelings not being acknowledged. Especially, once we were living internationally, doing so was easier than continuing to rock the boat, so to speak. At that time, I was trying to squeeze out as much joy from my marriage as I could. Until I couldn't.

Both suppressed and repressed trauma make you numb to situations that you would not usually accept or tolerate. Because you bury the hard feelings to get through your worst moments, you can't see that they still affect you. These forms of trauma blind you to the long-term reality of the damage you are doing to yourself, in order to manage your life in the moment.

I know I lived too much of my life on autopilot, unaware that the unthinkable treatment I endured from Howard and the desperate escape I was forced to make still lived within me. I thought I had to—I had two precious little ones to raise in a world that didn't always understand them. My perfect, beautiful, mixed-race babies kept me moving forward, whether I was ready to move on or not.

CHAPTER 3

Black Baby Doll

I got pregnant at nineteen. Out of wedlock. By a black man. In the South. In 1985. Can you imagine?

You may say, "Wow, what a challenge." But I say, "What a gift!" I truly believe that. This pregnancy completely changed my life, and me, for the better. Not once did I feel like, "Oh shit! What the hell have I done?" None of this was negative in any way for me. I knew I was meant to be pregnant with this baby.

I can't say the same for those around me. People made that abundantly clear. The looks Howard and I would get walking the streets in the French Quarter! Racism was rampant. Even well-meaning people would ask, "How are you going to manage having a child out of wedlock?" and "Aren't you scared to have a mixed-race child? Your baby is going to have a difficult life."

But I was not concerned. I loved my baby so much, and I had no doubt that I not only could, but *would*, provide it all. I knew I was carrying a girl from the start. I just knew it. I felt it. I kept telling myself, "I'm going to raise her to be independent. If she sees a pair of earrings she wants in the window, she can buy them for herself. My girl is independent, beautiful, and caring."

And I was right. Ashley's essence is beauty, grace, and elegance. She has been that person from birth. She is a compassionate, caring woman. And independent! And, dare I say…way smarter than I ever was at her age. She has the ability to find in herself all that I have so often sought outside of myself. I wanna be just like her when I grow up!

I was also very lucky to have a healthy baby. The day I found out I was pregnant was the only time I saw a doctor until I went into labor. I wasn't raised with money, and I didn't know anything about ultrasounds or prenatal vitamins. The women in my family have a long history of having healthy, strong babies, and they taught me to trust what my body needed. Some might say, "Well, not your mom, if you were born a preemie." But it was the fierce, tenacious *fuego* I was born with that helped me survive in 1965, weighing only 4 lbs, 3 oz, without the help of a Neonatal Intensive Care Unit (NICU).

I ate what my body craved and rested when my body wanted. It was honestly the healthiest time in my life. But I recognize that a million things could have gone wrong, and we were so lucky that Ashley was healthy. Another blessing.

I always saw my kids for who they were, not for the color of their skin. Still, racism was very present in our lives. I always saw other people's judgment as their problem, not ours. But it was still a fact that my skin looked different than Ashley's and Elijah's. That was something we had to navigate as a family. Especially after I married my second husband, Roger. Roger is

Dutch and very Caucasian. He used to joke that when he stood against a white wall he would disappear. He would refer to our family photos as a Benetton poster—each model representing a different ethnicity. And no joke! We really did look like it! But we loved it.

Luckily, our little family experienced very little overt or violent racism. The people who condemned me and Howard for walking through the French Quarter as a biracial pregnant couple didn't make the same comments to our kids. But there were definitely hiccups along the way and tough conversations that needed to be had.

The first hiccup arose quickly. When Ashley was five, she asked me about our different skin colors. That was the first conversation we had about race. We were in Ocean City, vacationing with Howard's family, and I was the only person there who wasn't black. Ashley ran her two little fingers up my forearm, and then she ran the same two fingers up her forearm. She asked me why my skin was different. I didn't get it at first, so she did the gesture again and asked a second time. It completely caught me off guard. And then it clicked! I was the only white person in the house. Of course I looked different from everyone else. And she had noticed.

I explained to her—as well as I could to a five-year-old—that people have all kinds of different skin, hair, body types, etc., but inside we are all the same. We all experience the same feelings. We all have bones, organs, and a heart. I looked her in the eyes and said, "Sweetie, we come from different parts of the world and speak different languages, like English and Spanish.

Some of us have light skin like Momo's (my mom was a light-skinned Latina), some of us have your beautiful olive skin, and some might have Daddy's skin color."

She blinked and replied, "Okay, Mommy."

I went on, "We all have different colored eyes, but different colored eyes still see the same." I rubbed her forearm, then mine, and added, "It doesn't matter because we are all the same inside." Pointing gently to her little chest, I knelt down to her eye level and softly said, "We all bleed red blood." I wanted her to understand the concept of equality in a way she could grasp at her young age.

I continued to explain as best I could that we are all created equal and are just as important as the person next to us. She sat and listened and looked at her skin and mine throughout the conversation. I could see her little wheels turning. When I was done, she smiled and said, "Okay." And that was that! What had been a huge and nerve-wracking conversation to me was such an easy concept for her.

On some level I always knew I was going to have this type of conversation with my children, I just didn't think Ashley would be so young when the conversation was had. It is still one of my all-time favorite conversations of my life. Ashley handled the content so maturely. That is who she has always been and still is today. I have said it before and I will say it again. I want to be just like Ashley when I grow up!

One of the first things I had to learn as a mother of black children was how to take care of their hair. Ashley's in particular was a challenge for me. Her hair has always been beautiful but quite different from mine. The texture and the type of curl was something that I had never styled. I had no idea what to do with it. Ashley spent most of her young childhood in braided pigtails. As she got older, I learned more about caring for black hair and the cultural importance of black hairstyles.

One morning before school, while I was sitting on Ashley's bed and braiding her pigtails, she told me she wanted to get a relaxer. She said that some of her young classmates were already getting relaxers, and she wanted one too. The strong chemicals in relaxers at the time frightened me, which was why I was against using them for her at such a young age. For those who don't know, a relaxer is a chemical treatment that smoothes the hair to produce straighter hair with less frizz. When she turned twelve, I took Ashley to a salon, but I wasn't willing to completely give up our hair-care bonding time. So, I learned how to apply a relaxer myself, then taught her when she was old enough. These days she wears her hair long and natural. And it is absolutely gorgeous!

As a young mother of mixed-race children, I knew from the beginning that I was going to deal with racism. It propelled me to become aware of my morals, integrity, and inner beliefs on race. It became a catalyst for raising loving, caring, confident individuals with the inner knowing of their lineage and the personal value that comes with it. Have you experienced any of the -isms? Sexism? Racism? Are you experiencing an -ism now that you need guidance on? If so, this book is for you. My formula will give you the wisdom needed to deflect any -ism that may impede on your life.

Despite a lack of overt racism in our family, ingrained biases would sometimes surface. For Christmas one year, I bought Ashley a Water Baby. Do you remember those dolls? They were a big hit when they first came out in the mid-eighties. You filled their body cavity with water, and it made them feel natural, flexible, like a real baby would feel.

Water Babies were available in white and black skin tones. I got Ashley a black baby doll, because she's half black. The doll looked like her. When my mother saw it, she was so upset. She had never expressed any racist comments about my kids, and her ex-husband, my stepfather, was mixed-race. Her anger made no sense to me. Even to this day, I don't really understand it.

The only conclusion I can come to is unconscious biases formed in the generational gap. She may not have believed that her half-black granddaughter was any less beautiful than a white girl, but I think being raised in an era when that sentiment was common ingrained a belief that white dolls were simply more acceptable. I think she thought that white dolls were the standard, and never thought about why. Or maybe she thought that if Ashley could choose to see herself in a black or a white doll, she'd have an easier life identifying with the white doll. I really don't know.

We fought about it to the point that we didn't speak to each other for days. I was upset and confused. Dumbfounded, really. I had been so excited that there was a doll that resembled Ashley. And she loved that black baby doll!

My mom and I eventually stopped talking about the doll so we could keep the peace. Then, one day after family dinner, my mother brought it up again. So, I sat down across the dining table from her, and we discussed it. It was the same argument over and over again.

Finally, I asked her, "Why did you give Melissa a Spanish speaking doll for Christmas?"

You see, around the heyday of Water Babies, another popular doll came out. She was kneeling, wearing a white nightgown, hands together in prayer. She, too, came in different skin tones, and she could pray in English or Spanish. My mother had chosen a white, Spanish-speaking doll for my niece Melissa.

She replied, as though it was the most obvious thing in the world, "Because she's a Latina."

I simply said, "Exactly."

I actually saw the light bulb go off in my mother's head. The "ah ha" moment, if you will. She leaned back in her chair and said that she hadn't thought about it that way. I think it was the first time my mother realized some of the things I had to deal with as a young mother to mixed-race children in the South. My babies have been loved by my entire family since day one, but it was the first time my mom was aware of the difference in raising our children.

That conversation with my mother was uncomfortable, but it was nothing compared to the first time I had to sit Elijah down to discuss race. Trayvon Martin, a seventeen-year-old black boy walking home from 7-Eleven with Skittles in his pocket, had been fatally shot by George Zimmerman, a white Hispanic man who felt threatened by Trayvon. I was forced to have THE racism conversation, the one every mother of black children, especially black boys, dreads.

As the mother of a black, Hispanic young man, I felt I had no choice. I had to tell my son that in the world we were living in, it was possible for something like that to happen to him. To be careful, to be alert, to be smart. To never give anyone a reason to see him as a threat. Trayvon had done nothing but walk, but unfortunately, it was in the wrong place, at the wrong time, with the wrong person around who had the wrong mindset. As a mother, a human being, I will never comprehend anything about that case. My heart goes out to his family, even today. Thankfully, Elijah never experienced violence because of his race. At least, he has never shared any such experience with me, and we have always shared a lot.

All in all, the concerns, thoughts, or worries that others had about my having mixed babies didn't really materialize for my children. Or me. At least not in the extreme ways that I feared. Maybe the comments Howard and I received as a pregnant biracial couple caused me to expect a meaner world for my kids than the one they got. Or maybe times had slowly changed and we weren't affected by them all that much. Ashley was teased in elementary and middle school for being too light-skinned, too "caramel," to sit with the black girls. Our family received snide stares and curious comments from ignorant people. But luckily, neither ever escalated to violence.

Still, the comments hurt. But through it all, my babies remained the same. It never changed how they saw others, regardless of race, ethnicity, religion, or color of skin. I believe this mindset came from the way my babies were raised. From day one I raised them to know—not believe, think, question, or wonder, but to KNOW—that we are all created equal in God's image.

I learned this truth from my mother. Even though my five siblings and I had three different fathers between us, we never thought of each other as half-sisters or half-brother, separated by our different dads. NEVER. We were family. Period. That's how our mother raised us. Her love, care, and compassion knitted us together into one family. I think this is true of humanity. We are one family. Therefore, it is not our place to look down on, to belittle, or to judge anyone. That's not our job. Never has been. Never will be. At least not in my little family that I have created for us.

Do not ever let anyone make you feel less than. Never let anyone make you feel small in your own skin. You are perfect as you are. And don't you make anyone feel less than. Do not make a person feel that they are less important than you, because that says more about you than it ever will about anyone else.

I always made sure my kids knew that I am grateful to have black children. To have had the opportunity to learn more about the African-American culture and history. To eat soul food! And yes, even to care for Ashley's hair. I have traveled and lived in several places throughout the world, and I think I enjoy that as much as I do because of learning more about my children's culture. It sparked curiosity. I consider myself blessed to have biracial children because they have opened my eyes and piqued my interest about other ways of living. My biracial family has been such a blessing!

The first time I tasted soul food was at Howard's Aunt Dorothy's house. She could throw down in the kitchen! This time, it was collard greens and ham hocks. I had never had them before. I mean, why would I have? They're not part of my Latina culture. But let me tell you, if you haven't had them before, you are missing out. Absolutely delicious! If made right, the collard greens will melt in your mouth like cotton candy. And ham hocks add such a rich smoky flavor to any dish. I'm now known for occasionally throwing them into my New Orleans red beans and rice. So, so, so good! Both of these foods were born of slave oppression: Collard greens were one of the only vegetables black slaves were allowed to grow for themselves, and ham hocks, the joint between the pig's leg and foot, were one of the only pork cuts deemed undesirable enough to be rejected by the white elite and so given to slaves. These slaves took the undesirable castoffs and turned them into some of the best recipes I've ever tasted. I learned so much from my black family about the incredible tenacity of my children's ancestors. I am proud to be their mother as they continue such a legacy.

I also learned about the hardships of being black in America, the ways that African-Americans are rightfully exhausted by having to be those tenacious fighters. My children are black, and as their mother I had to educate them on the injustices that have played out in our society against their race. I have had to advise them. At times I have had to console them. I had to educate myself to be able to do this, and my heart is heavy with all that I have learned. An injustice on one black individual is an injustice on all African-Americans. It is an injustice on the black race as a whole. That goes for any race. As I have said, we were all created equal.

We as parents take on the issues that our children are faced with. We want to protect them. But there comes a point when we have to step back and give them space. Space to take what you've taught them and fly. Space to learn on their own. Space to make mistakes. Watching my children get hurt by others, especially in regards to their race, has been incredibly hard. But watching them make mistakes and hurt themselves? So much harder. It amazes me sometimes that with all I've been through, I didn't become the helicopter mom. Yet, I was able to resist becoming that parent. Growing up with five brothers and sisters, I learned very young that you can't save everyone from pain all the time. And you shouldn't. It's not your lesson to learn, and it's not your mistake to make.

CHAPTER 4

Not My Mistake to Make

I was the second youngest of six siblings, so I heard a lot of grown-up conversations very young. My older siblings often discussed teenage things in front of me, like dating, breaking rules, and rebelling against our parents. There was a seven-year gap between my next-oldest sister and me, so I think the older kids thought I was too young to understand. Or maybe they just didn't realize that I was always listening. I still am. Even now I pay attention to my surroundings—observing and listening. That impulse may come from this family dynamic.

With such a big gap between my siblings and me, whatever I was experiencing at any point in time, I was alone in this. No one could really relate to the raw emotion of my pain, concerns, fears, or even excitement. Anything I went through, my older siblings had gone through and learned from years ahead of me. They could never quite remember how some childhood pains stung, since they already had acquired the insight and wisdom that I had not yet developed. My younger sister was years away from experiencing any of what I may have been going through.

She couldn't be the confidante I needed either. I wonder if I made her feel the same way.

I guess this is when I started to feel that it's always been just Me, Myself, and I...when I started to feel like I had to be my biggest supporter. Don't misunderstand me—my coming from such a large family meant there was always someone to talk to. Even if they could not always relate to me, my siblings did their best to be there for me. But even their best was so far from where I was in life. I had to make up the difference. I was the only one walking in my shoes.

Where do you fit in your family? Is childhood when you started to feel alone?

One day, one of those young-adult conversations took a dangerous turn. At least, it felt dangerous to me, so much younger and not yet in that teenage rebellion phase. My older siblings were getting ready to go out and meet some friends at the lakefront, and I was, as always, hanging around unnoticed. They were talking about their plans for the night and the friends they would meet. And the boys.

My sister, Elizabeth mentioned that her ex-boyfriend, Orlando, would be there. The other siblings let this comment slide by. But I was distraught. She was not allowed to see Orlando.

She and Orlando had lived together for a bit of time. All I knew about their history was that she had broken up with him a few months ago and moved back home. But I knew that he was bad news. Our mother had forbidden her to see him again, and his name was spoken with an air of danger. I later learned that Elizabeth left him because he put his hands on her.

As I mentioned, I was young and not yet privy to the details of what actually happened. But even without the details, I was worried.

My siblings piled into the car and headed off, unconcerned as usual about my eavesdropping. I was too young to understand, after all. But I wasn't too young. I knew that my sister was breaking the rules, rules that were there to protect her. I feared that she might get hurt.

It affected me so much that after they left to meet their friends, I paced the side patio of our house. I don't know how long I stewed there. Back and forth, back and forth, from the front of the house to the back. I know it was a long time. That *fuego* within me had me pacing. I felt like I knew a dirty secret. I knew she was making a mistake.

In the pacing back and forth, I kept coming to the same conclusion. What control do I have in the situation? What influence do I have? The answer was quite simple: None. I had no control or influence. I was a child, and I didn't understand her perspective. Eventually, I came to the conclusion that "it was not my mistake to make." And I have lived my life by that. For me, it was one of those moments where you shrug your shoulders and go on with the rest of your day. You might ask why I didn't tell my mother. Because I am not, nor have I ever been, a tattletale. Growing up, none of us siblings were. We respected each other too much for that nonsense, and we always had each other's backs. Most importantly, though, it was because she was going in a group. I chose to trust my siblings to protect her.

In the end I was right in continuing on with my day, because I do not recall his name being mentioned again. That was the last time I heard him come up in any conversation amongst my siblings and their friends. She was okay after all.

This mindset taught me accountability. The mistakes I have made throughout my life are mine and mine alone. There were some choices I made in my older siblings' footsteps, even though I had seen them not work out. Even knowing the outcome, I made my own mistakes. I had to—that was how I learned. My greatest lessons came from my own mistakes in life. And I, only I, own them. I take accountability for each and every one.

As I look back on my life, the first major mistake I made was not necessarily meeting and marrying Howard. I learned a lot about life in that relationship, such as what people will do to you if you allow them to. No, it was the acceptance of his lack of respect and his abuse, the length of time that I allowed it to continue. That was my mistake and mine alone. I accept complete accountability for it all. It was my decision. I had my reasons for staying, which were, in the end, the exact reasons I left: my children. Talk about coming full circle, right?

I've raised my kids with this mindset too. As difficult as it is as a parent to let go, to let our children make mistakes, there comes a time when we have no choice. There were times that I knew my son or daughter was involved with someone who was not a good fit, but I would keep that opinion to myself. They had to learn like I did. I have always been there for them, no matter what. I am there when they need me for advice, direction, a hug, and even a laugh. That will never change. Motherhood ignited a passionate parental *fuego* within me. But they have to learn their own life lessons through their own mistakes, not from a lecture given by me. Though, I am sure Elijah would say I lecture.

When my second husband, Roger, and I got the opportunity to move from Orlando, Florida, to California with his employment at Disney, we were offered a relocation package for a family of four. Ashley and Elijah were adults in their early twenties, but they could have come with us. Ashley was in a relationship with a young man and made the decision to stay behind in Florida with him. That's not the way she presented her decision to us, but I knew. Elijah made the decision to stay in Florida as well, because he didn't want Ashley to be alone in Orlando. And he had a life and friends of his own there.

I knew Ashley's relationship was not going to last. I am not going to get into any personal details because it is not my place to say, but the one great thing he did was to give Ashley a male boxer puppy that came to live in our home at two months old. Ashley named him Kobe—after Kobe Bryant, of course. We all came to love him dearly. I will always be grateful to him for that because Kobe was a complete joy to have. He was such a great dog! And Ashley's first "baby."

Of course, Ashley's relationship ended soon after we moved. And not on good terms, as I recall. Both Ashley and Elijah have said to me, several times, that they regretted not moving to California with us. They could have possibly had the opportunity to live internationally with us, too. Who knows? I thought from the beginning that it was a mistake for them to stay in Florida. My mother's intuition told me that man was not the one for Ashley. But I had to let it happen. I had to let them figure it out.

It was my responsibility to teach my children everything I could so they could make their choices with as much wisdom as possible. I had to set the consequences for their choices. But the choice was always theirs. Their mistakes were theirs to make. I don't think I have ever said to them, "It's not my mistake to make." It's not my place. They'll learn that for themselves.

Mistakes are yours to make. Every choice is your own—just be aware that each one has consequences—good or bad.

And you, my friend? Have you ever found yourself in a situation where you had to realize that it was not your mistake to make? Letting your loved ones make the wrong choices is not easy. I've gotten a lot of gray hairs in the process. But like most difficult things in life, letting go of control can be quite freeing for you as well. It can be a teaching tool for all involved—dare I say—for you as well.

CHAPTER 5

White Knight in Shining Armor

I was a single mom taking two buses to my job as a hostess in The Grill Room of the Windsor Court Hotel in downtown New Orleans. One day, I walked into the Suite Service office to say hello to a friend when I saw a gentleman sitting at the desk. He was facing away from me, wearing a white dress shirt, blue dress slacks, black leather shoes and black leather suspenders. *Smart dresser*, I thought. I spoke with my friend for a few minutes, then walked back to my hostess stand in the restaurant.

The phone rang.

"Thank you for calling the Grill Room, you've reached the hostess stand," I answered.

But it was not a customer on the line. It was my friend in Suite Service, gushing that the man in her office wanted to ask me on a date. I didn't even know his name.

"Roger, his name is Roger," she said.

I stood there and could not think of one reason not to go on the date.

So I answered, "Why not?"

Twenty minutes later, Roger approached the hostess stand, introduced himself, said he had noticed me right away, and asked if I would like to go out to dinner. Of course, I said yes.

I had a good time on that date. We talked about everything but mainly family. Of course, we discussed my two young children and my being a single parent. One thing that was consistent during the meal, and many others to come, was Roger's heavy accent. Roger is Dutch, and I distinctly remember having to ask him to repeat himself several times throughout the evening. Imagine Arnold Schwarzenegger's accent when he first came to the United States. That was how thick Roger's accent was when we first met. As the years went by, it became less and less pronounced, to the point that I didn't hear it anymore. Eventually, it went away. Or maybe I just got so used to him.

Roger worked long hours as the Suite Service Manager of the Windsor Court Hotel, eventually getting promoted to the Maitre D' of The Grill Room. A Maitre D' is the person that oversees the restaurant staff and ensures that all operations run smoothly throughout the evening. He would greet guests, ensure they enjoyed themselves, were content with their meal and experience, and were satisfied with the overall restaurant atmosphere and experience. Between his working hours, my morning shifts at The Grill Room, and the kids, we had little time for dating.

My dates with Roger were usually late night dinners after Ashley and Elijah went to sleep. I would make sure they were fed, bathed, and read to, which I did every night, then put them down for the night. Then Roger would pick me up, usually for a night at a swanky New Orleans restaurant. Roger loved to impress with his knowledge of wine. He would typically order bottles of several different types of wine, depending on what our entrees were, sometimes one for each course. It didn't come across as wanting to get me tipsy but more so as his wanting to impress me. And it did. Extensive knowledge of anything is a sexy trait, as is an accent.

Roger was such a refreshing change from the typical type of man that I would date. He was a great person with a life and profession of his own. His career, I knew early on, was very important to him—a significant part of who he was as a man. That was extremely attractive to me. Roger is Dutch and, other than Latino men, I had never dated someone who was born and raised in another country. That was very appealing to me too.

We fit together effortlessly from that first date. There was rarely a day that we didn't make each other laugh. A sense of humor is incredibly attractive to me, and Roger's dry humor was exactly my flavor of funny. Plus, we respected each other, especially when it came to his career and my being a single parent. He was kind, generous, supportive…and I was having so much fun. Still, I had some walls up. I was not going to let myself fall in love. Ashley and Elijah had to be my priority.

One evening I had to cancel our dinner date because I had come down with a nasty cold. I was lying in my mother's bed watching TV when she walked in saying someone was here to see me. I dragged myself into the kitchen, and there was Roger.

Keep in mind I looked like shit. I felt like shit. And I didn't give a shit. I couldn't even give a shit that he was going to see me looking like shit. Like I mentioned, I didn't feel good.

Roger had brought a bunch of groceries. The items he unloaded from the grocery bags had all been thoughtfully purchased: medicine, throat lozenges, soups, oranges, orange juice, strawberries, crackers, lemon tea bags. As he unpacked the bags, he explained why he had selected each item and how he thought it would help me. He emptied the last few items—yogurt and Oreo cookies for Ashley and Elijah, along with a bottle of red wine, and a rose for me—gave me a hug, kissed my forehead, and said his goodbyes. I watched him pull his white Ford Galaxy out of the driveway.

Suddenly, he stopped and got out of the car.

He gave me one last smile and said, "I'm your white knight in shining armor."

Then he drove off.

I don't know how long I stood there in the doorway after he left, a good five minutes at least. Mind you, a few of my neighbors were hanging out in front of their homes, so there was a chorus of "oohs" and "aahs" as he drove away. I was in shock. I think that was the moment I fell in love with him. It was the act that broke my determination not to fall in love. Up to that point, raising my children had been my only priority, my one and only focus. I was not willing to split that focus.

Have you ever experienced that? Have you had tunnel vision for your life, and something or someone came along and changed it all?

Roger changed it all for me. He was my knight in shining armor, after all. Support became a big part of the foundation of our relationship.

For many years we had quite a wonderful life together, a lovely marriage, and a beautiful family. Roger helped raise my kids. We had a few marvelous years in New Orleans. Then he got a position with Disney World, and with it came money, travel, and decades of incredible opportunities. We lived in South Africa, Florida, California, Tokyo, and Paris. Over the years, our homes contained a lot of love, laughter, joy, and happiness, and our life was full of adventure. Let me tell you—when it was good, it was amazing!

But after twenty-four years of marriage, and all the challenges that come with a long-term marriage, especially a marriage that had its issues…tension had taken a seat at the dinner table.

It was a slow change. Roger was always a supportive husband and stepfather but not always in the ways I wanted him to be. Too often, his career came first. I knew from the beginning that Roger's career was very important to him. In fact, that was one of the qualities that drew me to him. But he struggled to find a balance. Often his work overshadowed our home life, our family life. There were times he would bring magazines to Elijah's basketball games and read them in the bleachers. The looks and comments the other parents shared! At the time, I was just happy that he was physically present, even though he wasn't always fully invested with his time. But over time, the pattern stung. That was difficult for me both when we were married with kids at home and once we became empty nesters living internationally.

Over twenty-four years, he became more successful, and we slowly pulled away from each other. By the time we were living in Paris, we had become companions. We had been going through the motions for so long that it had become the norm. Roger seemed to be fine with it, but I wanted more for myself, more out of my marriage, more out of life. Even if I didn't always feel like I deserved more…I wanted more. More joy, more peace, more passion.

There was another problem that plagued our marriage. I suspect, even with his denials, that during our twenty-four years of marriage there was an affair or two. Some emotional and others physical, I think. I have my reasons for believing so.

When we were living in Orlando, I had a gut feeling for weeks that things were off. I couldn't put my finger on why, but something told me to look in Roger's wallet. I didn't know what I was looking for, but I found it anyway. I found a woman's business card in his wallet with a personal note written on it. It expressed her being happy and thankful for his time and attention. She ended her little note with: Love, Karen.

After I let Roger know that I found it, I left. I stayed the night at a friend's house, and when I wouldn't come home, Roger packed a bag. He went to Saint Augustine on a business trip for a couple of weeks. When he came back, we went to marriage counseling. It took months for us to work through the distrust that came from that card. Through it all, Roger never admitted to an affair. Of course, only he knows the truth. It is something I can never know for sure. Though it never sat right with me. But I loved him. We were a family. A part of me didn't want to rock the boat. It was easier to keep my head in the sand, so to speak. I have to wonder if the antidepressants I was on played a part in keeping me docile. Maybe I was too numb to realize what a big deal living without trust was.

After we had moved past that particular situation, I later found a box in the garage that Roger had brought home from his office. Inside, there were several cards from this same woman, including a birthday card and one that reminisced about a fun Sunday afternoon on his Harley Davidson.

Interesting, right?

Looking back, I don't think Roger could help himself. He loved being the knight in shining armor too much to resist helping a woman in need. There were countless times that he would explain away my intuitive suspicions with the assurance that he was just helping someone out, being a good guy. The "someone" just always happened to be a pretty woman. And honestly, whether or not any of these connections were physical, I don't think he was lying about that part. He loved to be needed.

While we were living in Orlando, Roger took on the role of general manager at the beautiful Grand Bohemian Hotel—a place where modern elegance blended effortlessly with classic and eclectic touches. It became even more special to us when, years later, our daughter Ashley and son-in-law Steve chose it as their wedding venue. During Roger's time managing the hotel, they hosted an extravagant New Year's Eve party in the lounge. I was excited to spend the evening by Roger's side, imagining us ringing in the new year together in his element.

But just before midnight, Roger unexpectedly pointed out a young, blonde cocktail waitress working the event. To my utter disbelief, he told me that she had been driving our black Infiniti around town for her personal errands over the past few weeks.

Excuse me?! This was brand new information to me. I had thought our car had been sitting in the hotel's underground parking garage all this time. I had no idea that another woman had been driving it around as if it were her own. I was *livid*. Without a word, I left the party immediately, fuming with anger. By the time midnight struck, I was alone in the car, speeding down the highway.

I don't know why Roger chose this moment to reveal this to me. The only reason I can think of is the possibility of her thanking me for it in some way during the evening. Or her mentioning it to me? I don't know. Having worked in the hospitality, service and retail industries I try to make it a habit to acknowledge anyone who works in these industries, preferably by their name (I like name tags). Maybe he felt guilty and wanted to clear his conscience. Whatever his reason was, I don't think he expected me to receive the news and leave as abruptly as I did. But for me, that revelation marked the beginning of a major shift.

The evening before Elijah's eighteenth birthday, we took Elijah and a friend of his to a tattoo parlor a few blocks past The Grand Bohemian. Elijah had always wanted to get a tattoo, and

Roger and I had agreed he could have one for his eighteenth birthday. Roger dropped us off in front of the tattoo parlor and left to find parking. Elijah, his friend, and I went inside. We were immediately told that they did not tattoo anyone under eighteen, no exceptions. It did not matter that he had a parent's permission and would be eighteen in a few hours. They were not going to give him a tattoo, period. We left the tattoo parlor disappointed, several hours earlier than expected and decided to wait for Roger on the sidewalk.

Outside the shop, a crowd of people was walking down the sidewalk toward us. Roger was with them. He must have run into them after parking the car. He was talking with a pretty petite brunette, and they were so engrossed in their conversation, smiling and laughing with each other, that he walked right past us. He did not notice his own wife and son standing right before him, or the fact that he was walking past the tattoo parlor where he was supposed to meet his family. I was shocked—he had just left to park the car a few minutes ago, and now he was too absorbed in conversation with this woman to see his family! Mind you, the woman was running her hand up and down his back, and he did not seem to mind. I later learned she had been thanking him for settling her hotel bar bill when she couldn't pay. He was such a good guy, but I was left invisible on the sidewalk.

Then there was the time when we lived in Japan. All foreign executive cast members were assigned Japanese interpreters for business meetings. The interpreters were men and women, and they rotated often. The Japanese love to discuss business over dinner, especially while drinking. Roger would typically drive his assigned interpreter from the office to our apartment and park in the building's underground garage. He would bring the interpreter upstairs, drop off his briefcase, make a brief introduction, and give me the opportunity for greetings. Then Roger and the interpreter would Uber to their dinner meeting.

One evening I realized it was past the time that Roger normally would stop by, but he was nowhere to be seen. Again, my intuition was saying something's not right. I went downstairs to check whether our car was in our parking spot. And it was. I touched the hood and it was still pretty warm. He had just been there! Why had they not come up? Why didn't he want me to meet this particular interpreter?

Late in the evening, once Roger got home, I asked him why he hadn't come up before his dinner meeting. He was lying in bed, clearly signaling that he didn't want to discuss it. After some prodding, he said that he didn't bring the interpreter up because he was protecting her.

"Protecting her? From what?" I asked.

"From you."

Roger said I made this interpreter uncomfortable. Though he didn't say why at the time, I later learned that this was the interpreter who had crossed a line a few months before (more on that story in a future chapter), and I had addressed her behavior as inappropriate.

I was shocked. I always welcomed his interpreters into my home, and I had handled that particular situation well. More importantly, why was his gut instinct to protect this woman and not his wife, who had been disrespected by her in the first place? I was highly offended, and it takes a lot to offend me. But mostly I was hurt. Once again, I was hurt by the actions of my husband toward me because of his concern for another woman. And my gut was right. This interpreter ended up causing more problems for our marriage down the line.

After these and other experiences, my trust in Roger was difficult to nurture. It was one of the reasons we separated when we later moved to Paris. I left him there and lived alone in the States for several months, contemplating the future of my marriage. Eventually, Roger and I decided to give it one more shot. I moved back to Paris, and we committed to saving our marriage. We even discussed and agreed on doing marriage counseling.

I had been back in Paris for a couple of weeks when a nagging feeling led me to check Roger's phone. Things had felt off between us lately, and I couldn't shake the suspicion that something was going on. That's when I found several texts from a younger American woman he worked with. In one message, she asked if he had sent her a care package, which included a packet of American-brand taco seasoning—a rare find in Paris. Roger replied that he wasn't the one who sent it, but he'd love an invitation to dinner so they could cook an American meal together.

I was absolutely flabbergasted. We were just beginning to put our marriage back together! He had never mentioned this level of friendship or familiarity with the coworker, despite promises to be more open and forthcoming. And he obviously knew her address. The familiar tone even made me wonder if he had been to her house before. And the audacity of inviting himself to dinner at her place! Not him and his wife, just him. Sharing a hard-to-create, much loved, sentimental, homesick meal together. I was so shocked that I had to read the texts over and over again. At some point I noticed the timestamps and realized he had been sitting next to me, in the living room, on the sofa, while they were texting. I had a hard time wrapping my brain around the secrets and lies.

In each of these situations, I was made to feel like I was overreacting. I was the one being unreasonable.

Do you think I was being unreasonable? How would you have felt or reacted in one of these situations, much less all of them?

Throughout the years, our home had been filled with love and laughter. Roger had always supported me and my kids. But these situations kept occurring—moments when my feelings, thoughts, needs, wants, and concerns were not considered in the face of other women. They didn't matter to Roger. That became blatantly obvious throughout the years. It seemed the "white knight" in him needed to continuously rescue a damsel in distress, even when it hurt his wife.

When I found the text in Paris, I kept that secret to myself for a couple of weeks. I gave myself the space, grace, and time to evaluate how I felt about it. It was the first time that I allowed myself to sit with the knowledge, the feelings, and the pain without reacting. In that space, I finally admitted what I had known in secret for years: Roger was a White Knight in Shining

Armor ... but not just for me. He would keep being that knight for other women. And I was not okay with that.

From meeting and dating in New Orleans, to traveling the world together, Roger and I lived a fairytale life. To this day, I am asked how I could walk away from that. In the end, Roger forced me to acknowledge that he had developed a pattern of being involved, in some way or another, with other women. Affair suspicions aside, he consistently put other women's needs before mine. His wife. It was a pattern that had become a thread throughout the fabric of our marriage. His unwillingness to put me first caused arguments, distance, and pain each time that I was made aware of it.

What made this all so incomprehensible was that we were actively working to rebuild our marriage. We had just been sitting together on the sofa, flipping through pictures of model homes we dreamed of building or buying. Yet, at the same time, Roger was texting another woman about sharing a sentimental meal with her. That spoke volumes. It was the final straw— the moment I realized I couldn't continue down this path any longer.

All the traveling around the world, all the Prada bags and Louis Vuitton purses, the exquisite jewelry, the fancy dinners... all these perks made life lovely on the surface. But they are not my love language. I was not being seen. I was not being heard. I was not acknowledged. I was definitely not being appreciated. No wonder I was depressed.

Again, my tenacity got the best of me. For the last few years of my marriage, I kept thinking and hoping that if I kept trying to make it work, it would. As time went on, I was losing bits and pieces of self-worth. Fighting over his attention then recommitting to our marriage became such a relentless cycle that I completely lost myself in the process. Again, my choice. My decision. I take full accountability for staying longer than I should have. In losing myself, I lost sight of my value as a mother, a wife, and a woman. I allowed that to happen. I did that. Thank God I am not that same person today.

In Paris, I hit a breaking point. I finally admitted to myself that no matter how good my life with Roger looked, I was meant for more. I'll share more about that realization in Chapter 8. We divorced shortly after, and I moved out of Paris. Back in Florida, I began a journey back to myself.

I gave myself time and space on that journey, and I leaned into my desire to change the parts of me I did not like. In that process, I learned the tools to work on myself, which led to the creation of my EIF. And to who I am today.

I have not spoken, nor will I ever speak, a bad word about Roger. He doesn't deserve it. He is a good person with a kind heart. He is a great dad to my daughter, Ashley, a wonderful opa to my granddaughter, and he is kind to my son, Elijah. He was a great provider while we were married, even if not necessarily in the ways that I needed him to be. But it is my story, after all, and I have chosen to speak my truths about facts that happened in our marriage and how they affected me. But sharing my experience does not mean I blame him. I don't.

During our very cordial divorce, we spoke often about wanting to remain friends, and we were, at first. I will always continue to wish him much happiness. Always.

If you have experienced or are experiencing not feeling heard, valued, acknowledged, and appreciated, you are not alone. Please love yourself enough to do the work and follow my EIF. I promise—you will not regret it. I don't. I don't look back on any of it with regret. This relationship and my complacency with its faults have played a major role in who I am today. And I love myself more today than I ever have.

You will too.

CHAPTER 6

South African Delights

South Africa is such a beautiful, serene, and spacious country. The wildlife, as I'm sure you can imagine, is majestic. In 1992, Roger was given the opportunity to be part of the opening team for The Palace Hotel in Sun City in Bophuthatswana, South Africa. The best part? He took me and the kids with him!

Sun City is a self-sustaining resort, with its own bank, medical center, shopping plaza, restaurants, water parks, small grocery store, and more. It even had a discotheque! As resort residents, we had full access to everything—the resort itself was basically our backyard. My knight had taken me to paradise. The best way for me to describe my life and experience living in South Africa would be to compare it to a modern-day version of the movie *Out of Africa*. Have you seen the movie? It is one of my all-time favorites, along with *Under the Tuscan Sun*. It might be time for a remake of them both. Don't you think?

South Africa's seasons are opposite of the United States. In North America, we celebrate with BBQs and bikinis on July 4th, but it's winter in South Africa in July. It can get pretty cold in the evenings in the winter months. It took a few months for us to adjust to this seasonal difference. South Africa's landscape also varies significantly during summer and winter months. Its terrain consists of rivers, deserts, coastal plains, mountains, plateaus, and savannas. Depending on the season, the country can be cold, dry, brittle, and dusty or lush, hot, tropical, humid, and full of greenery.

I can't imagine the life I would have had if not for this opportunity. It would have been less colorful, that's for sure. Yet, when Roger first got the job offer and asked me to join him in South Africa, I turned him down. It was a big ask! We weren't married yet, and Ashley and Elijah were comfortable in Holly Heights, the same neighborhood where I grew up. We lived with my mom at the time. We had support, family, and friends all around us. Plus, I didn't have a strong desire to live in Africa. Could I uproot my life—my *kids'* lives—to be with the man I loved? Again?

For our next date, Roger cooked a beautiful meal for me. When I arrived, the table was set with a delicious spread: Paella, a fresh tossed green salad, French bread with butter, and dessert. But alongside the meal was something unexpected—a pile of pamphlets about South Africa. These weren't about tourist attractions or fun adventures; instead, they were brochures for daycare centers, grade schools, and potential job opportunities for me—all in Sun City, South Africa. At the time, our children were still very young—Elijah was just three and Ashley was five years old. Roger told me he loved me and said the only way he would accept the job offer was if the kids and I came with him. If I didn't go, he promised he'd turn it down.

We were in love. There was no doubt about that. The kids loved Roger, and he loved them. My heart was full. I asked Roger if he was sure this was what he wanted, and his response was an emphatic "Yes!"

I told him I would only come if we were going to get married one day. I'll never forget his response. He stated that he didn't need a ring on his finger to be serious, loyal, and committed to our relationship. I responded that I didn't either…for me. But that was not how I wanted to raise my kids. If I was going to make the decision for my kids and me to cohabitate with a man, it was because we were a family. Not because Mom was playing house. I am not opposed to couples living together before marriage—both Ashley and Elijah have lived with significant others at one time or another. It's just not something that I wanted for myself as a single parent.

After a few glasses of wine and a lot of discussion, we agreed that the kids and I would go to South Africa with the understanding that, in time, Roger and I would get married. Roger moved to South Africa before we did. He had to settle into his new position, and I had to wait for my divorce from Howard and child custody to be finalized.

I went to visit him for a couple of weeks while we waited on the paperwork. It's a long twenty-four hours of travel—two flights to get to South Africa, with an additional couple of hours by car from the airport to the Sun City Resort. Most of The Palace Hotel area of the resort was still under construction, so Roger was living in one of the other hotels in Sun City. Still, even through yellow tape and orange cones and unfinished concrete, I could see the stunning property it was going to be! While Roger worked, I toured the resort, spent time relaxing at the pools, and chatted with other expats living at the resort. It was the first relaxing vacation I had enjoyed since becoming a mom. Roger's intention was for me to see that we wouldn't be living in a hut with mud floor and roof…mission accomplished!

Next door to The Palace Hotel, a crocodile farm had been converted into a visitor-friendly park, with walkways above the crocodile habitats, a building with incubators and housing for baby crocodiles and other reptiles, and a small cafe. The crocodile farm was basically an open-air structure. The cafe had an extended deck with roofing and overlooked the farm landscape of the crocodiles' habitat. South African to the core. I loved it! During my first visit to the crocodile farm, colleagues of Roger who had become friends took me to breakfast. It was the morning after we all enjoyed a night of dancing at the resort discotheque (I really wish I could remember the name of it but unfortunately I don't). While at breakfast, I held a snake. I had a long-sleeved sweater on and the snake slithered into my sleeve for warmth. It's the one and only time I've held a snake. I don't know if it was the *fuego* in me or because I was in South Africa or what, but doing so felt like a completely normal thing to do. Has there been a time when you have allowed yourself to experience something that you normally wouldn't do because you were in another country, or state, maybe on vacation? That's what the crocodile farm experience was for me.

One afternoon during the crocodiles' afternoon naps the park's manager, Brandon, with whom Roger and I had become friends, took us down below where the crocodiles lived. The fact that Brandon stayed close probably made me feel comfortable enough to make that journey. We walked around among them while they slept—they were hibernating. I'll admit it was nerve-wracking, but I was too awed to be scared. I was very aware that I was having an experience of a lifetime.

The farm's pathways above us started to get crowded with observers, guests watching what we were doing below. The gasps, the "oohs" and "aahs" I heard from the crowds above reiterated the rarity of the opportunity. As quiet as we were trying to be while the three of us walked around in the grass among them as they slept, the snap of a branch on the ground or the crunch of leaves sounded louder than it should. If they heard you, their heads snapped in your direction along with the upper part of their bodies while emitting a low, slow growl. Till this day it remains one of the most exhilarating experiences of my life. Plus, Brandon was always nearby with a large, long, bamboo stick in case they needed to be whacked if they moved toward one of us. And believe me, a couple of times they got whacked! Hard!

That trip was the perfect taste of Sun City: shiny and new, luxurious, convenient…but still very much part of the South African wild. I was sold. Ashley, Elijah, and I moved to South Africa once my divorce from Howard was finalized and I got full custody. The four of us had spent a lot of time together while Roger and I were dating, even before we made the decision to move to South Africa. By the time we were all living together, Roger and the kids had already begun forming a strong bond. Ashley and Elijah were so excited about the move because they knew it meant we'd finally be a family with Roger. They absolutely adored him, and the idea of living together in South Africa felt like the start of something new and wonderful.

But! We missed our original flight to South Africa and ended up flying out the very next day. Ashley, who was seven at the time, cried her heart out at the airport. She was devastated, missing Roger already. A family friend had helped me earlier that morning by driving me to the airport to drop off all of our luggage and boxes—a massive task, given that moving with two young children was no small feat. They then dropped me back home and returned later to take us to the airport for the flight.

Unfortunately, they misjudged the traffic and were late picking us up, which caused us to miss the flight. I believe it could have been divine intervention, a moment to remind us that even with the best-laid plans, sometimes things unfold on their own timing.

I worked in the only jewelry store in The Palace Hotel, Charles Greig Jewelers. One of their brochures happened to be on Roger's coffee table the night he asked for us to go to South Africa with him. It is a family-owned jewelry store with over one hundred years of history. In case the obsession with shoes didn't clue you in, I love jewelry, and this job definitely had its perks. I held in my hands loose, large-carat rubies, emeralds, diamonds, and sapphires. I was surrounded all day by beautiful necklaces, earrings, rings, and bracelets that were made with all the stones and metals you can imagine. That autumn, Roger bought my engagement ring there.

Roger proposed marriage to me during our first Christmas in South Africa. It was Christmas Eve, after the kids had opened a small gift from under the Christmas tree and had been put to bed, and we were enjoying an intimate glass of wine. One minute we were sitting in the living room listening to music… the next minute Roger was down on one knee with a ring box in his hands. And with the Tiffany-style ring I had been admiring while I worked at Charles Greig Jewelers! I wasn't expecting the proposal. It was a magical holiday, even if we did have to order our Christmas trees in August to ensure delivery in December.

One evening that following April, I grabbed the calendar off the kitchen wall and told Roger to "shit or get off the pot!" And that's how our wedding date was picked! Writing the words on paper sounds pretty cold, but in reality we laughed and had fun picking the date. The next few weeks were a whirlwind of wedding preparations—from choosing the venue (The Palace Hotel, of course) to selecting the florist (also from The Palace Hotel) and finalizing the menu (courtesy of The Palace Chef, naturally). I even took on the challenge of designing my own wedding dress. This involved finding and hiring a local seamstress to help me select the fabric, lace, and other materials, and then crafting the dress itself. My fittings were always at home, which made it increasingly tricky to keep the dress a secret from Roger. His curiosity was hard to contain.

The dress turned out beautifully. To add a personal touch, I found someone who created invitations with specialty paper.

Roger took it upon himself to address them by hand using a fine-point calligraphy pen, teaching himself calligraphy from a book as he worked. Imagine that! And, in a special twist, we were the first couple ever to be married at The Palace Hotel.

By the way, I still have the dress. I picked every aspect of that dress—from the material, to the lace trim on the sleeves and collar, to the overall design: a floor-length, form-fitting mermaid gown with long sleeves and a high, round-neck, swoop front collar. The back of my dress was cut low to show off my bare back. That is the only thing about my design that my dressmaker asked me to reconsider in one of my fittings. She wanted me to go lower and show more. I reconsidered and met her halfway knowing that I had designed a bolero jacket to wear later in the evening for the reception. I still have both of my wedding dresses. I imagine my granddaughter, Mia, playing dress up while wearing them one day. I can actually picture it; I see it in my mind's eye. And it brings a big cheesy smile to my face.

We celebrated many fun occasions at the resort. The Miss World Pageant was held at The Palace Hotel three years in a row. During our years in South Africa, I had the opportunity to meet several celebrities, including Christie Brinkley and Grace Jones, which was quite exciting.

Ashley's eighth birthday was a dream come true for her, featuring a gourmet cake crafted by The Palace Hotel's renowned pastry chef. We had a bouncy castle and a variety of small animals in two petting pens. The birthday party theme was either circus or zoo-related, neither Ashley nor I remember exactly. The majority of the decorations—all in that cute and colorful animal theme—were a gift from one of the ladies who worked at the Charles Greig Jewelers Johannesburg location. My daughter remembers this party vividly and still talks about it today. As her mother, that is extremely special and important to me. A happy childhood memory.

We also had some amazing adventures outside the resort. One day, Brandon, the crocodile farm manager, took us on a private off-road safari. We saw several of South Africa's main animal groups: cheetahs, leopards, zebras, buffaloes, giraffes, and elephants. We got so close to an elephant that the men in the group climbed out of the truck to get a closer look. I stayed in the truck with the kids, because Roger was concerned for our safety if we approached as well. They were huge!

We also took a road trip down to Cape Town through Kimberly, known as Africa's diamond country. We realized on this trip that the tribes still follow the old ways. We saw a young man running in tribal garments and full body makeup. We were told that he was going through an initiation into manhood which they must do alone for several days. It brought the difference in culture to the forefront of my mind. The kids were young at the time, but that made an impression on them.

In South Africa, students are in school year-round; they attend class for three months, then have a month off. At the end of the month, they go back to class for three months, and so on. We as a family loved it! I have never experienced it in any other country. We preferred it because it permitted us to travel on longer trips during that month off that was given once in all four seasons.

It was time to shop for school uniforms for the next school quarter which was during summertime. I drove Roger's cherry-red 1968 California Special Mustang with the white racing stripes down the front hood, his pride and joy and a real treat for the kids. On a gorgeous summer day with bright sunny weather, my hair blowing as I'm driving with the windows down, feeling blessed to be living the experience of South Africa, we headed to Rustenberg—maybe thirty minutes from Sun City on one of the rare occasions that I would drive outside of the resort.

Suddenly, sirens! The police were flagging us down. Imagine the horror I felt when a tank, complete with rifles and machine guns, pulled up behind us! It wasn't the police, it was the military! I can feel heart palpitations just thinking about it!

The kids and I got out of the car and stood on the side of the road. We were terrified, confused, alarmed, and just as curious about them as they were about us. There were a few seconds while we all stood there on the side of the road looking at each other before anyone spoke. During those few seconds while my heart raced, I did a mental checklist of all the legal documents I had on me that were required for the car being allowed to be driven in South Africa, as we had it shipped internationally from the States—the kids' and my passports and my license proving I had authority to drive in South Africa. But then the soldiers asked if they could check out the car. That was why they pulled us over! They had a blast admiring the car from top to bottom—they even sat in the driver's seat in their uniforms, proudly posing with their machine guns. Too bad there weren't any cell phones back then, as that would have made for a great picture. But, hey, it makes for a great story.

That car got a lot of attention on the road. Heck, even when it was just parked at the hotel, there were times I would find people admiring it, peeking through the windows and checking out the car's original features. Especially the vintage-car lovers. That Mustang traveled with us to South Africa and back to the States, just too precious to leave behind. But shortly after we moved back to the States, Roger decided to sell it. It broke my heart to see him have to let it go, but we were living paycheck to paycheck at the time with two young kids, and he decided the funds could be used elsewhere. To this day, I still think about the Mustang from time to time. I've always had a soft spot for cars—whether it's the different styles, muscle cars, or V-8 engines. Admittedly, Corvettes were never really my thing. Instead, I've always been drawn to the classic Ford Mustang muscle cars. Their vintage style remains timeless, and it's definitely the tomboy in me that's still enamored with them.

And I think of the man who sold his pride and joy to support my kids. Despite everything else Roger was, he was always *that* man.

One day while we were still in South Africa, Roger came home and said that President Pinochet of Chile would like to have lunch the next day. I was excited for Roger, until he clarified, "No, he wants to have lunch with *you*." Evidently, President Pinochet had asked if there was anyone who lived in the resort who spoke Spanish. You guessed it! Me. I was the only person who spoke Spanish.

So I met him for lunch the next day. When I arrived, the restaurant was completely empty except for President Pinochet and a few of his higher-ranking military men. I was escorted to his table, not by a hostess or server, or even the restaurant manager, but by one of his right-hand men. I know he is a controversial figure, but to me he was a gentleman. The conversation flowed easily, he was kind, well mannered, polite, and thoughtful even. The conversation was mainly his asking me what life was like in Sun City for me, as a Latina woman. At the end of the meal he told me that if there was anything I ever needed to let him know. Of course, I thanked him and said that it was very kind of him to offer that. And that was it. Lunch was over. It was an experience of a lifetime, obviously. I'm writing about it thirty years later.

My life returned to "normal" after that. Well, the normal that comes with living in South Africa from 1992 to 1994, which was during the political tension that came around the time that Mandela was elected President.

On his inauguration day, Roger served as the captain of the team of waiters from The Palace Hotel that catered the inauguration luncheon. During the event, a member of Mandela's team approached Roger with a special request: could the Palace Hotel team prepare dinner for Mandela and his family at their private residence? Roger was ecstatic about the opportunity. At one memorable moment, President Mandela was seen trying to eat while simultaneously feeding one of his grandsons who was perched on his lap. Roger approached and asked President Mandela if he would like for Roger to feed his grandson so he himself could eat. And so he did. He fed one of President Mandela's grandsons while he sat on President Mandela's lap. Roger received a lovely photograph of the occasion, which I later had matted and framed for him.

By the time Mandela won the election, the political atmosphere had changed from a pot of simmering water to a full boil. We had overnight bags packed at all times, and the American Embassy had military helicopters ready to pick us up on the golf course if it became necessary. Thankfully, the embassy didn't need to resort to that, but there were a couple of times when it got close. Roger sent the kids and me back to the States early for our safety, then joined us at the end of the year.

In South Africa we bonded as a family through all the new experiences we were having individually, as a newly married couple and our shared family experiences. Our daily routines were organically created, such as bed times, rules, homework, etc. Roger, Ashley, and Elijah created their bonds and relationships with each other as child and parent. Roger and I continued to become close in a way that made it easy to work as a team in parenting and creating the foundation of our little family. As volatile as the political situation was in South Africa at the time, it was a wonderful and happy time in our family bubble.

Looking back on my life I can honestly say this was one of the happiest times. Living in Sun City, South Africa, was such an amazing experience! The adventures we had there cannot be experienced anywhere else in the world. But, they were not my final adventures abroad. A few short years later, Roger and I moved again—this time, to Tokyo, Japan.

CHAPTER 7

Utsukushii—Profoundly Beautiful

It was during my time in Japan that spirituality first began to resonate deeply within me. The country holds a special place in my heart because of this profound experience, so much so that I chose to name this chapter "Utsukushii." This Japanese term captures the essence of profound beauty, transcending mere appearance to evoke a deep, emotional response. It signifies a beauty that touches the heart and soul in a way that feels both profound and transcendent, and that is exactly how I feel about my time in Japan.

Roger and I moved to Tokyo at the end of 2011, just nine months after the devastating 9.0 magnitude earthquake on March 11th. Despite our natural apprehension, we had always dreamed of visiting Japan. The culture had long intrigued us, and this was our chance to immerse ourselves in it.

At this point in his career, Roger had been working with Disney World and Disneyland for a number of years. He had been promoted and transferred from Disney World to Disneyland in California, where we lived for eighteen months, when the opportunity with Disney Tokyo was offered to Roger. He was promoted from the General Manager of the Anaheim Disneyland park to the Director of Operations and Director of Food and Beverage of all of Tokyo Disney.

One Tokyo Disney perk for expats was membership in the Tokyo American Club. It was a very prestigious club. Gorgeous in all aspects. We enjoyed spending time at the gym, eating at the many restaurants—both casual and fine dining—attending events held there, swimming in the pool, and, most importantly, making friends with other expats. For me the best part was the gymnasium. I found community there: a group of individuals who were just trying to connect with like-minded people. We would meet twice a week to play indoor volleyball. It was my savior! I played indoor and sand volleyball growing up, so it was definitely a stress reliever, a way to connect and make friends with other expats, and I was pretty good at it. And we were competitive!

Shortly after moving to Tokyo, Roger and I came up with a code word for when we didn't understand something about the culture: interesting. We often would say to each other, "That is *interesting*!"

The most "interesting" thing to me about Japanese culture is the Gaijin Hunting Season. Gaijin is what the Japanese call someone who is a foreigner. Gaijin Hunting Season typically starts around March and continues through the summer. It's when single Japanese women basically "hunt" or pursue a Gaijin male. And ladies, it didn't matter if he was married and had children. It. Did. Not. Matter. What mattered was that the Gaijin men met the criteria of a high level of education, prestigious titles, and substantial wealth. When summer arrived, these women would make their move. While the families were away for the season, leaving the men alone in Tokyo to work, the single women would pursue them, hoping to win them over. Often, this pursuit ended as nothing more than an affair, and many times it led to broken families. What do you think? Does that qualify as something…interesting?

As for me, I didn't go home for the summer since we were empty nesters. However, I did encounter an unusual situation. One of the Disney interpreters—the same one Roger hadn't brought up to the apartment before his dinner meeting—asked if Roger could dress up as Santa Claus for Christmas so that the women in the office could sit on his lap for photos. Naturally, I declined the request.

She proceeded to ask that, if they would charge per photo and give me a cut, would I reconsider? My response was "Absolutely not!" Can you believe it? She had the audacity to ask me in front of Roger, and she did so several times. For those wondering, Roger's response to the interpreter was something like, "Why are you involving my name in this?" What would you have said if it were you in my shoes? As you can imagine, the proposition did not go over well with me. Oh, and by the way, the Japanese do not celebrate Christmas. They decorate everywhere for the season, they have Christmas sales and shop extensively during Christmas, but Christmas is not part of Japanese culture. Isn't that…interesting?

Within my first couple of days of living in Tokyo, I experienced my first of many earthquakes. I was barely awake, very jet-lagged, about to enjoy my first cup of coffee of the day. The ground beneath my feet moved—literally moved—for several seconds. It was more of a sway than a jolt but still very unnerving. I froze. I was stuck trying to comprehend what had just happened. It didn't take long for it to register, and my first thought was *I will never get used to this*. There are forty to fifty earthquakes *daily* in Japan. I experienced several, and while I didn't completely get used to the phenomenon, I understood that most are more of a sway than a jolt.

Two big ones do come to mind. For one of them I was babysitting my friend's one-year-old daughter at their place on the twenty-first floor of their apartment building. The noise of the glass panes scraping against the metal window frames sounded like nails on a chalkboard, only much louder. The building swayed in wide arcs, and the emergency alarm blared in the background. The baby looked at me with sheer terror in her eyes, and the thought of how I was going to get us, along with the family dog, down the twenty-one flights of stairs overwhelmed me completely.

The most frustrating part of that experience? The emergency announcement on repeat in the building was only in Japanese! I did not understand a word of it!

I experienced another earthquake, but this time I was sitting in our living room watching TV. Just as I noticed Max, our mixed terrier, had dashed between our sectional and sofa table, my world began to sharply jolt, sway, jump, and fall—seemingly all at the same time. We had a free-standing bar whose three large shelves held several bottles of a variety of wines, liquor, champagne, liqueurs, mixers, and all the glasses required in which to serve them. Because Roger was the Director of Food and Beverage for Tokyo Disney, the bar in our home was properly and professionally stocked at all times. The clear and eerie sound of glass clinking, tinkling, clashing, and crashing was unnerving. Both our dogs—Max the terrier and Noodle the dachshund—must have thought the world was ending!

I looked over to see the light fixture above our dining room table sway to the ceiling from end to end, dramatically, from left to right, right to left, left to right. I could barely stand once I got on my feet. Walking three feet seemed impossible. The dogs were barking at my feet, nervously trying to maneuver the ground beneath their little paws. It felt like an obstacle course getting to the front foyer. I had just managed to get my coat on, and was on the floor putting my boots on when the shaking suddenly stopped. And that's where Roger found me when he walked in from work. The best part? Roger didn't feel a thing! He was driving on the highway the entire time.

I would be remiss if I didn't add here that Max and Noodle absolutely loved living in Tokyo. They continued to be incredibly spoiled. And not just by us. As you can imagine we tended to travel a lot, especially throughout Asia, along with trips back to the States and Europe to visit family. The majority of the time we took the dogs with us, but on the rare occasions that we didn't, our housekeeper would stay in our apartment with them until we returned. That's when they really got spoiled! As you can imagine, extra walks, extra treats, and a little extra food served to them each meal. Max and Noodle were both individually amazing dogs, but even more so together as brothers, and they were loved by all.

Tokyo is a city that is easy to get around in through the extensive train system, by bike, or on foot. As crowded as Tokyo is, there are gorgeous, unique little parks tucked in various areas of the city, and all, if not most, are dog-friendly. The Japanese, as a whole, love their dogs. And they tend to treat their domestic dogs as family. There were numerous times while walking through the city I would pass a stroller and there was a fifty/fifty chance it was transporting a child or a dog. Not to mention the number of doggie boutiques scattered throughout the city was mind boggling! Gourmet dog food and treat boutiques, dog clothing and accessory boutiques, grooming boutiques, with manicures and pedicures included. Max and Noodle hit the jackpot!

I have to admit the clothing boutiques came in handy during the winter months. Max and Noodle had never experienced snow or that degree of cold weather. So the clothing boutiques came in handy because yes…I bought them each a winter coat and winter booties. Laugh if you want, but once they got used to wearing them, they were grateful for them. Before their winter coats and booties Noodle refused to go out in the snow for walks or to do his business. He would huddle against our apartment building finding a little break in the bushes where he could hide and relieve himself. Once he got used to walking in his coat and booties, he strutted around the city like he was the main dog. Max was always cool from the moment he was first humiliated by having to wear them.

Traveling throughout Japan was a beautiful experience. The scenery is stunning. I have never seen so many shades of green. Even in the heart of the city there's greenery everywhere. Walking throughout Tokyo was where I first came to feel a hint of spirituality. As I mentioned at the beginning of this chapter - spirituality knocked on the windows of my soul because I was unaware. If it had knocked on the door of my soul; I would have answered. It's weird to say but as packed and crowded as Tokyo is, it's where I first began to feel a connection to nature.

Our apartment building was right behind the Intercontinental Hotel, whose back street is lined on both sides with full-grown cherry blossom trees. During cherry blossom season, we were blessed to be able to walk right out our front doorstep and step right into a world of pale pink loveliness. And the views from our apartment windows…stunning! We lived across the street from a graveyard that was hundreds of years old and still fully functioning. Japanese graveyards are quite different from American ones. The graveyard, with its headstones, statues, trees, flower arrangements, and a couple of small benches, along with its winding pathways, looked absolutely stunning when covered in snow from our apartment.

Over the three years I lived in Tokyo, the graveyard became a sacred place for me. I observed that the Japanese honor and celebrate their loved ones who have passed away by visiting them on holidays, incorporating them into their festivities. Holidays like Mother's Day, Father's Day, Children's Day, and Grandparents Day were especially significant. Families would dress appropriately for these occasions, often gathering together to bring food, beverages, gifts, and decorations to the gravesites.

It was a touching sight. I would watch long enough to appreciate the beauty of their traditions before stepping away to respect their privacy. I felt privileged to witness this moving practice that truly touches the heart. Did it soften yours a little? I hope it did.

You would think I would have felt the same connection to nature in South Africa, with its vast open landscape. But it didn't happen to me there. Actually, I had a very hard time sleeping when I lived in South Africa. It's also where I first started to experience migraine headaches. I would need to be under the covers in complete darkness and complete silence, completely still. They would last for hours (felt like days) until they eventually faded away. I remember speaking to our nanny in South Africa about not being able to sleep and her immediate response was "the land here does not like you." I was taken aback. I think it's more likely because of the high altitude in Sun City. But what could I say? Maybe the altitude sickness was South Africa's own way of telling me it was not my true home.

But I digress. The first time I experienced feeling anxiety within my own skin was in Tokyo. It was a typical day, and I was at our apartment. Only the dogs and I were home. Disneyland Tokyo is an hour outside of Tokyo, so Roger was gone most weekdays until early evening.

Despite the familiar surroundings, I just couldn't get comfortable. Sitting, standing, walking the dogs. It didn't matter. My anxiety was at the utmost highest degree. I had never felt it that way before. It was the first time I asked myself, "What is wrong with me?"

What's wrong with you?! I had a very blessed life. A great husband whom I loved, and who loved me. Two adult children whom I adored. What in the heck was going on with me? Why all this anxiety? What was WRONG with me?

Looking back on it, I now believe that walking through Tokyo and adjoining prefectures, traveling throughout Asia, in general, experiencing all of the natural beauty, the history of their culture touched my spirit. It initiated an awakening I wasn't yet aware of. I think my inner intuition was starting to realize that my soul was meant for more, my mind was rejecting that idea and asserting that my life was perfect, and my body was responding to that cognitive dissonance with extreme anxiety.

Knowing what I know now, this is where I would have applied Step One of my EIF, and continued through to Step Four of my EIF, and I would sit with myself in silence. But I did not know this then and so I couldn't. I was not capable. I swept the anxious feeling under the rug. Unbeknownst to me, that pile under the rug would eventually kick my feet from under me. But I didn't know any better at the time.

It was my mistake to make...and I made it. Ha!

Tokyo is such a lush city in the sense that they have little parks full of green landscaping, trees, bushes, plants and flowers in crooks and crannies tucked in throughout the city. Even though Tokyo is one of the most congested cities in the world, the serenity I often felt within myself walking through the streets, the beautiful shrines and their gardens with such amazing history going back centuries, unbeknownst to me, had started to awaken the stirring of my spirituality.

The different types of flowers! Gorgeous! I saw beautiful flowers that I have not seen in any other part of the world. I am not a botanist, but I do enjoy plants and I love flowers. I got my green thumb from my momma.

But I digress. I truly believe that my spirituality was knocking on the windows of my soul when I lived in Japan. I did not know it then, did not realize it. You will read more, my friend, further in my book on how my spirituality came to be. Is your spirituality knocking on the windows of your soul? What would that feel like, you ask?

For me, it showed up as depression, anxiety, and many, many sleepless nights. They all played a role in my sitting quietly in silence as I have asked you to do. It is the first step of my Emotional Intelligence Formula that changed my life. It is also what brought me to such a point of inner peace that I was not only able to meditate but to benefit from it immensely.

The first trip Roger and I took after we moved to Tokyo was to Seoul, South Korea. We went with two other couples who both had young children under the age of two. It was a last-minute trip for us, but we were really excited to travel throughout Asia.

First, let me start by saying that I highly recommend traveling to South Korea. I had no expectations, but the city, the food, and the people…the entire experience surprised me. The people of South Korea were so kind and endearing, especially the children. It remains on my bucket list of places I want to revisit. I will go back some day. The city is beautiful, clean, and more modern than one expects. We spent our time walking the streets, visiting monuments and eating. There was a lot of eating, and everything was delicious! I remember one night when we picked a table in one of the sections of the Gwangjang Market where there were a lot of mom-and-pop vendors. The guys would come back and forth with all kinds of food from the different vendors. It was all divinely tasteful.

At one point, I peeked over the side of the concrete half-wall next to our table to see what I can refer to only as a plastic kiddie pool full of soapy water and dishes. Yep! You guessed it. That's where all the plates, pots, and pans were being washed, by hand. Not the most sanitary. Even so, I distinctly remember feeling a punch to the stomach, and immediately after…a sense of…I don't care. I still highly recommend going. I would go and do it again. It was an experience of a lifetime!

We also went to the Demilitarized Zone, which borders North and South Korea. It was a long ride by tour bus—several hours to get to the location. We immediately knew when we were close because we could clearly see where North and South Korea's military huts were situated facing each other with soldiers at the ready, rifles in hand. Literally facing each other. I can't put words to the feeling when seeing this, even today. As we pulled into the area where it's located there were trees and picnic tables—a mini arcade park, if you will. There was even a roller coaster. As the bus pulled into the park, we could see families sitting at picnic tables, eating. The tour guide told us that this was where families came to "share a meal" with their loved ones who were living in North Korea.

My heart shattered at the thought. It was beautiful and devastating all at the same time. I couldn't even begin to imagine what it must be like for them. Can you? The sorrow? The longing to just share a meal with a loved one, yet knowing you couldn't. Once inside, we toured caves South Korea had found that North Korea had built trying to infiltrate their territory. These caves went on for a while, and the farther we went, the smaller the space became. We walked in a single file to a spot where we could see the entrance to North Korea's side within twenty feet. At one point, I distinctly remember feeling like I was crouching a good bit to continue to get through. I turned back to look at six-foot-two Roger wondering how in the hell he was managing the tunnel. He said he was okay, but it's a mental picture that I will never forget. We only did half the tour because children were not allowed in the second half, and we wanted to stay with our friends. We were able to walk around and even snapped a picture or two with soldiers standing on guard, which was allowed as long as you didn't touch them. There was a section with telescopes facing the North Korean countryside. North Korea had set up a fake town with electricity and all. Looking through the telescopes you could clearly see that the town was fake, but it probably looked convincing at night from above.

As we walked out of the building, there was a chain-link fence lined with framed photographs of families, individuals, young and old. These were photos South Koreans had placed as a shrine of their family members living in North Korea. I immediately felt heartbroken and thankful to be an American.

One of my favorite spots in Seoul was the Cheonggyecheon area. It's a stunning location where concerts and performances are held, surrounded by vibrant lighting, art, and beauty. The blend of modern architecture with historical landmarks—featuring ancient wood, carved stone, water elements, and lush greenery—creates a breathtaking scene.

On clear days, with the sun shining bright, the inner-city park transforms into a delightful space. A large area is dedicated to water spouts that spray cool water onto children running around, blowing and chasing bubbles, their laughter filling the air. It remains my favorite memory of the entire trip to South Korea and still brings a smile to my face.

Walking through Cheonggyecheon, it's easy to forget you're in a bustling city. The elegance of the area provides a serene escape from the urban hustle. My favorite time to visit is at night, when the lighting, energy, and ambiance create a completely stunning atmosphere. Bukchon Hanok Village gives you a nice feel of living in a typical South Korean village. The children enjoyed the freedom of walking and running around. They also got a lot of attention because of their blue eyes and blonde hair. As you can imagine, these traits are not common in Korean culture.

Of course, South Korea was not the only country I explored during this time of my life. During our three years living in Japan, Roger and I traveled throughout Asia, often as a perk of his position. When Roger had to do a site visit to Hong Kong Disneyland for a few days, we extended our stay to enjoy Hong Kong for ourselves. It is one of the most hot and humid places I have been to on the planet. No exaggeration—within three minutes of stepping outside you are covered in sweat. I am a Latina, and I have traveled extensively throughout the world. Very few places get as humid and hot as Hong Kong does. But the beauty of the city (especially at night), the vibrancy, and the Victoria Harbor skyline are worth traveling to experience. The skyline of Victoria Harbour is a sight that should be enjoyed at least once in a person's lifetime. And with its reflection off the water—gorgeous!

Singapore is beautiful! It is the most America-like city in Asia that I have been to. The vibrant colors, the food, the aromas, the modern architecture blended in with historical landmarks, and landscapes throughout the city are what set Singapore apart.

Thailand is a tropical gem. The people are lovely. It is a poor country, and you do drive through pockets of poverty. At times it's difficult to see because of the stark difference with its beauty.

The Philippines has a calmness to it; you cannot help but relax as you travel through the country roads. The rice fields adjoining homes, with ponds filled with ducks and livestock all within the same block, are majestic.

Bali is crowded, congested, and loud at times, with heavy traffic and crowded sidewalks, but Zen all at the same time. It is hot and humid nearly year-round. Having said all of that, it is also one of the most naturally beautiful landscapes that I have ever seen. The people are kind, endearing, joyful, always smiling and laughing. And the food is undeniably delicious! Regardless of your palate, there is something delicious to try and enjoy in Bali.

We were coming to the end of Roger's three-year commitment in Tokyo when Roger got promoted to Vice President of Disneyland, Paris. I think I manifested this because I had always said that I would love to live in Europe to be closer to Roger's family, to experience living in Europe, and possibly own a B&B in Holland some day. Wild dream, I know, but we had many conversations about it. On our trips to Holland, we stayed in castles renovated into boutique hotels or an old family farm renovated into a boutique hotel on gorgeous grounds, walked the cobblestone streets, visited old churches, and discussed living half the year there. And now we were moving to Paris, the City of Love.

CHAPTER 8

Paris...the City of Love?

Have you ever been to Paris? It is a magical city, especially at night. We were very fortunate to live in the inner ring of the Seine River. We lived directly across the street from Hôtel des Invalides, the military museum where Napoleon's tomb is. We had a balcony that ran the entire side of the apartment with a view of the Golden Dome of Les Invalides Museum to the right and a full view of the Eiffel Tower from every room except the kitchen and one of the two bathrooms. It was a typical Parisian apartment with original baroque hardwood floors throughout. Stunning! One of my favorite homes that I've lived in. The view of the Eiffel Tower was the cherry on top, especially at night. My daughter used to say the tower was her night light.

And the food! French wine, French champagne, baguettes, fresh fruit, fresh vegetables, beautiful flowers, all available from local markets a five-minute walk from our apartment. Who am I kidding?

Shopping in Paris was a dream come true—at least on the surface. I spent hours immersing myself in the city's beauty, searching for ingredients for meals, selecting flowers, browsing clothing, and exploring housewares. Every day was an adventure, from uncovering hidden treasures in the streets to visiting pop-up antique markets on weekends. The sheer luxury of it all was overwhelming, and I felt spoiled beyond measure.

And yet, despite living what many would call "the dream," I grappled with a deep-seated sense of emptiness.

I know my life sounds charmed. I traveled the world, living abroad with wealth and ease. Yet even as I wandered through the splendor of Paris, surrounded by beauty and culture, I felt a relentless anxiousness. The more I tried to fill the void with external pleasures—museums, travel, shopping—the deeper I sank into a state of numbness and anxiety.

The truth was, the beauty of my fantasy life was all external. The views, the food, the vibrant cultures: they were outside of me. On the inside, I was completely trapped and alone.

Parisian couples wandered the city, hands intertwined. I watched them from my window, just like I had watched those Japanese families bring flowers to the graves of their loved ones from my apartment in Tokyo. Yet no one brought me flowers. No one held my hand. My life had become increasingly isolating as I moved from country to country to support Roger's career. By this time, his attention was elsewhere, and my kids were back in the States. I was watching an idyllic life happen around me, observing joy, beauty, connection, incredible things very few people have the chance to experience, but I was a viewer only. I had no life of my own in these places.

I could feel deep down that something was missing. But what? The question frustrated me. I couldn't pinpoint what exactly I was lacking. I did not yet know that my unease came from within. While I immersed myself in museums, traveled across Europe, flew back and forth to the United States, and indulged in shopping, I still struggled with this sense of emptiness.

Then one weekend, I finally asked the question that had been on my mind for months. Roger and I were strolling through Paris, exploring pop-up antique markets—one of our favorite activities. We decided to take a break and enjoy a coffee at one of the city's beautiful hotel courtyards. I turned to Roger and I asked him, "Do you ever feel like you're meant for more?"

He responded, "No." He looked confused, like the question itself was crazy.

I continued, "Because I feel like I am meant for more. I just don't know what, and I don't know how to begin to figure out what the more is. I don't know who I am anymore, but I know I don't like me right now."

Looking back at that moment, that was a turning point within me. It took far too many years to realize that it was the pinnacle of the many times that I felt anxiety for what I thought at the time was for no reason. I had spent years uncomfortable in my own skin. And every time I felt this way, I thought I was alone. The only one who still didn't know who she wanted to be when she grew up.

Roger did not relate. As beautiful, magical, and romantic a city as Paris is, it was where our marriage ultimately fell apart.

I didn't know who I was, but I knew I didn't like who I had been here. If I didn't like myself, how could anyone else? If I didn't stand for something, did I fall for everything? As beautiful and blessed a life I was living, the beauty around me didn't hide the emptiness inside. And it had nothing to do with anyone else. Not Roger, my kids, my family, or my friends. It had only to do with me. It's not an easy realization to come to. For me, it took far too long—and I'm partly to blame for that. I can be overly tenacious, always striving to leave no stone unturned. I lived this way to avoid living with any kind of regret.

Unfortunately, this often meant I took too long to move on from situations, relationships, and other aspects of my life. I had a great guy, living in a beautiful city, shopping and signing receipts without looking at the totals. Some people's dream life, the lifestyle, the dream city…and I walked away from it all.

Living in the most romantic city in the world, I was lonely. The City of Love was not so for me. It was the loneliest time of my life.

In Paris, there was no American Club. The American Club played a crucial role in my social life in Tokyo. I had my own identity within my own circle of friends, a life apart from Roger's and my role as his wife. That did not exist on any level in Paris. I had no friends. Women my age were living a different lifestyle than mine. They typically had children living at home to look after. I, on the other hand, was an empty nester.

Plus, the French do not like Americans. They have no interest in you, your life, or what your experience as an American is like in their beloved Paris. It made making friends almost impossible. Yes, they are kind to tourists, but it is quite different to live there as a local from another country. I felt completely alone. I don't know if the atmosphere has changed much since COVID.

The majority of my time in Paris I entertained myself by walking the streets alone, eating meals alone, shopping alone, walking the museums alone.

Despite the loneliness of that time of my life, Paris has an undeniably special place in my heart. It may be the city where my relationship with Roger fell apart, but it is also the city where my relationship with myself began to heal. I am so grateful that I dared to ask that question: "Do you ever feel like you are meant for more?"

Roger may not have given the answer I wanted, but I found it in myself. Paris is where I finally admitted it: Yes. I am meant for more. It is where I began to realize that there was something missing within me. After all, if I couldn't be happy in Paris, then I couldn't be happy anywhere. The problem had to be me.

Perhaps it is the gratitude I feel for that realization that makes me remember my time in Paris so fondly. Somehow, when I think of Paris, I don't think of all the lonely afternoons. I think of my favorite museums and the gorgeous architecture. Sometimes, I even miss living there, almost like it is one of my many home towns. In some ways it is still a City of Love for me—the City of Self-Love. Despite the pain, it is one of my favorite cities in the world.

Paris is hard not to love, especially my all-time favorite landmark: Notre Dame. Yes, I love that cathedral more than the Eiffel Tower. Don't get me wrong, I love the Eiffel Tower! But no other landmark evokes the emotions in me that Notre Dame does. My favorite thing to do is to sit with my eyes closed in silence, basking in the fact that I am sitting in Notre Dame's beauty. I slowly open my eyes and take in all the wonder that is Notre Dame: the stained glass, the old pews, the statues, the history. I would miss my mother in those moments. She would have loved Notre Dame. I know she would. I can picture her sitting next to me in one of the ancient pews, eyes teary as she takes in Notre Dame's beauty.

    I am, after all, my mother's daughter.

CHAPTER 9

I Am My Mother's Daughter

When I was growing up, my mom cooked breakfast, lunch, and dinner every day. And I don't mean putting toast in the toaster. No, my mother would make different types of pancakes, huevos rancheros con frijoles negros, and arroz con leche, just to name a few. All from scratch. I would wake up to the heavenly scent of her zesting oranges for my favorite pancakes, her own recipe. They were perfect every time, light and fluffy with just enough bright citrus flavor. I have cousins who as adults still mention her pancakes. Or she'd make arroz con leche, a rice porridge made with condensed milk, sugar, cinnamon sticks, and, if you prefer, raisins. Delicious! So fragrant, it made the entire house smell divine. It was also one of Ashley and Elijah's favorites. I learned to make it for them, but mine was never as good as my mom's.

I can still see her in her brightly colored cute tops and capri pants, wearing one of her pairs of gorgeous shoes, looking so chic as she bustled around the kitchen or stood with her hip cocked in front of the stove. That is how she looks in most of my memories.

Mom never cooked from a recipe. I don't recall one instance where I ever saw her with a recipe in her hand. She had the natural talent of throwing together fresh ingredients in a pot or pan and turning them into a fragrant, delicious, satisfying meal. She had six children, and not one of us ever left the table hungry. Not once. I honestly don't know how she did it. I truly believe that cooking was her love language. And boy, did she love!

The ultimate expression of that love? Her Honduran tamales! My sisters and I would line up around the table, all of us girls ready to help mom with one of our all-time favorite dishes. We would all catch up with the ins and outs of each others' lives, laughing and chatting happily about work, husbands, crushes, school, while we worked creating her famous tamales.

Sometimes my aunts would come over to help, and the kitchen would fill with laughter and the click-clack of beautiful shoes. Mom would place two different types of masa harina and tons of filling ingredients on the table—rice, chicken, pork, potatoes, onions, tomatoes, olives, capers—all expertly prepared by her, of course. We would talk and tease while we worked, everyone taking responsibility for one of the myriad ingredients Mom put together. She would plop the masa onto a banana leaf and pass it on to the next person in line, who would add their designated ingredients and pass it on, and so on, until it reached the last person, who would wrap the tamale in the banana leaf, then add a layer of aluminum foil. As the tamale pile grew, so did our smiles. Not to mention the volume in the kitchen. We had to implement fun whenever and wherever we could. Mom was great at that.

My job was usually to harvest banana leaves. We had a banana tree in our yard, and my mom would hack the leaves from the tree with a machete. I still remember the day she passed that task to me. I was around twelve years old, and Mom called me into the kitchen. She described all the characteristics of the perfect banana leaf for tamales and where to cut them on the tree, then handed me her machete without any hesitation. It was almost as tall as me! But she knew I could handle it. I walked through our side patio, dragging the giant machete behind me. The sound of the blade scraping the concrete that day is one of my favorite childhood memories. Mom always believed in me, in that *fuego* burning inside me despite my small size. She trusted me to take care of myself, to get it done, and to pick the right leaves for her beloved tamales.

Beautiful. Strong. Graceful. Classy. Chic. Loving. Courageous. Kind. Composed. And of course… Tenacious.

These are the words that come to mind when I think of my mother. She stayed pure of heart through everything life threw at her, and let me tell you, her stories could fill a book even thicker than mine. At times she could be set in her ways, but overall she was fair. I often stood in admiration of her. I am definitely my mother's daughter, even named after her and proud to be.

My mother, Elba Hortencia, was born and raised in Tela, a small beach town in Honduras. All my life, I heard wonderful stories about Honduras. I heard about how beautiful the country is with its many mountains, lush greenery and flowers, tropical fruit, and quaint coastal beach towns. It is very poor, a third-world country. More than half of the population lives in poverty, and about a third—mostly women—live in extreme poverty. But the beauty of the country overshadows that. Honduras is a special place. Even the tasty corn husks cooked on the side of the roads throughout the country are beyond any other international treats I've tried, and I've traveled quite a bit.

The Honduran spirit is filled with tenacity, with a celebration of the beauty of life—even in hard times. We revel in the love and loyalty of family, friends, country, and heritage—all wrapped in an unquenchable joy. Mom had that spirit in spades.

When Mom was seventeen, her mother, my grandmother, got her a teaching job. Now, this would be her first job. The teaching position was further up in the mountains, where there was a one-room schoolhouse for all the children in the surrounding villages. The ages of the students varied from elementary to high school, all in the same room at the same time. They were the children of farmers, so they had to miss school regularly to help in the fields. My mother had no teaching experience, and the school had no resources to train her. Yet, she took the job, moved to the remote village on her own, and lived by herself—figuring out the job as she went, learning from experience as she always did. Amazing.

She would walk to the one-room schoolhouse every morning, her arms laden with books and materials for the lessons of the day. She wrote her own curriculum...her own curriculum! There was one particular young man who made a point to meet my mother on her walk to school every morning. He would take the books from her arms and carry them for her the rest of the way to school. He had a slight crush on Mom. I mean, who wouldn't?!

One day, she received a letter informing her that in one month a few government officials were coming to her school to administer a test to all the students. The letter clearly stated that each and every student needed to pass or they were going to shut down the school. But if all the students passed the test, the school would be supplied with new books. No pressure, right?

My mother spoke to the students and their parents about the significance of this test. It was very important to get the parents on board to keep the students in school instead of at work. She explained what closing the school would mean for their children's futures and asked them to commit to showing up in class every day and putting in their best effort to prepare for this test. She did the same; she committed her time, effort, and abilities as their teacher to create a study format that would help each child pass.

The day came when the officials arrived to administer the test. Every single student showed up. I don't remember how long it took for Mom to get the results. But when she did, she was ecstatic! Every single child had passed! My mother was still a child herself, and she had the tenacity to not only take the job, but succeed where no one had. Every. Single. Child. Passed. I was in awe of my mother at that moment. I was in my twenties when I first heard this story, and I struggled just to get Ashley and Elijah to do their homework. And here she had been such an incredible teacher at only seventeen. She was the original rock star in my book!

Today, I sit back and think about the strength and courage it would take, at any age, to accomplish all that, and I have nothing but complete admiration for her. I don't think I could do it today, let alone as a teenager. Could you?

A few years later, my mother left Honduras and moved to New Orleans, Louisiana, all on her own, without knowing the English language. She left my four older siblings in Tela in the care of my grandmother. She worked hard at three jobs every day while she saved every single penny to eventually bring my biological father, my four older siblings, and two of her younger brothers to America. I was born in New Orleans after she had brought them all here.

Unfortunately for my mother, my biological father became an alcoholic and was more of a burden than a contributor to the family dynamic. He brought problems, abuse, and headaches into my mother's life. In the end, she divorced him. She knew she could provide a better life for her five children on her own rather than with a man who only weighed her down. Ha! I am my mother's daughter!

She would eventually move on and marry a close friend of my uncle, one of the two younger brothers that she had helped move to the States from Honduras. They had my baby sister together. She went on to live a happy life with him for many years.

A piece of juicy gossip about this relationship: All our lives, my siblings and I grew up believing our stepfather was ten years younger than our mother. Fast forward to a few years after my mother passed, and we were having lunch with him. In the middle of a casual conversation, he dropped a bomb.

"You know, I was actually fifteen years younger than your mother," he said.

I nearly spit out my coffee and asked in disbelief, "What?! Are you seriously saying you're fifteen years younger than Mom, not just ten?"

"Yes," he confirmed. "I'm actually fifteen years younger than your mother."

He said it with a smirk on his face. I sat there for a moment, processing this surprising new detail, once again in awe of my mother. I felt a deep sense of admiration and respect for her. She knew exactly what she wanted and didn't let societal expectations hold her back. My mom was truly ahead of her time—a real trailblazer. She may have been the original cougar! Hot damn!

When I got a little older, Mom started sending me to Honduras for the summers. I spent every summer from ages thirteen to sixteen there, visiting my family, traveling the country, and making friends. I would stay with my Aunt Ondina in Tegucigalpa, the capital, for the majority of the time. Sometimes, I would spend a few days here and there with other aunts or at my grandmother's in Tela, the beach town where my mother was born and raised. My grandmother ran a small grocery store that took up a part of her house. It was located across the street from the telecommunication center that had the only telephones in the town. Whenever my mother called from the United States, I would be notified that she was on the phone and would have to cross the street, which was really just train tracks, to speak with her.

My grandmother, my mother, and my entire family were well known throughout Tela. Everywhere I walked, I would hear, "Elbita, como esta tu mama?"

Elbita—Little Elba. My nickname all through my childhood. Remember, my mom and I had the same first name. "How is your mother?" they would ask. More than half the time I didn't know who was asking. But they knew me. I was Elba's daughter.

I was taught to carry my passport everywhere. Back then, the military would drive around picking up children to join the army, no questions asked. As an American citizen, I couldn't be conscripted, but I had to prove it. I was told that it was vital to have my passport on me at all times. One particular evening, I was playing ball with my cousins and some neighborhood friends on the street a couple of blocks from my grandmother's house. Several military trucks pulled up a couple of blocks further down the street. We immediately stopped playing and ran toward Grandma's house. As we were running, my cousins asked if I had my passport on me, which I did. We later found out that no kids had been picked up that evening, but that they were doing their normal patrolling of the town. Whatever that meant.

One of my summers in Honduras, my Aunt Ondina asked me if I would like to stay. Believe it or not, I said yes.

I *loved* my summers in Honduras. I was spoiled while I was there. Each day, before she left for work, Aunt Ondina gave me one hundred lempiras—more than enough fun pocket money for anything I wanted to do. She was one of the most successful insurance agents in the capital. I had friends, fun, and money to spend, all in the most beautiful place I had ever seen. And the food! The sixteen-year-old me wanted nothing more.

Plus…the boys! Aunt Ondina always made sure to introduce me to the young men whose families she knew. They were sons of lawyers, doctors, businessmen, etc. They were always very handsome, educated, well dressed, and well mannered. And they drove nice cars. On one of my summer trips, I had barely walked in the door from the airport when the phone rang. It was a boy asking to speak to me. I asked him how he knew that I had arrived. He said that one of his buddies worked at the airport and had been on the lookout for me. He rang him as soon as he saw I was back. Talk about feeling special! Can you imagine the impression that made on me at sixteen? I mean, I clearly remember it all these years later. It's in my book.

I was ready to stay in Honduras forever. My aunt offered her home, and she had spoken to the director of the American School in Tegucigalpa, whose principal had agreed to reserve a place in the school for me. My education would be topnotch, and I would be taken care of. But when my aunt brought up the subject to my mother, she received a flat-out "no." Mom wanted me home. I was disappointed, but I thank my mother to this day for saying no. I can't imagine what my life would be like. Just knowing that I would not be the mother to Ashley and Elijah is enough of a blessing for me to be thankful that it didn't happen. That was the last summer I spent there.

I loved my time spent in Honduras and consider myself blessed to have been able to experience it as I did. Through those years of traveling throughout the country, I came to know the Honduran spirit. From the mountains, to the capital, to Tela, I began to understand that part of my mother's spirit, and through it that same spirit in me. I spent my nights sitting at my aunt's dining room table, or the table in my cousins' yard, playing UNO for hours and laughing until the stars came out. Just like Mom did. I enjoyed countless meals in my aunts' and uncles' kitchens, getting familiar with the different family dynamics and finding I had an easy place there. Just like Mom did. I got to be Elbita for a while.

She supported my leaving Howard, and, as I shared at the start of my story, the kids and I lived with her for months. She welcomed Ashley, Elijah, and me back into my childhood home with no questions asked. Mom took great care of Ashley and Elijah while I worked. It allowed me to work many hours and days, often weeks without a day off, without any worries or concerns regarding them being taken care of.

In her later years, my mom lived with my older sister Martha in North Carolina. I will always be grateful to Martha for that. What a precious gift to live a stress-free life in your golden years. I would visit to keep Mom company whenever Martha and my brother-in-law, Harry, went on vacation. I came to look forward to spending that time with Mom so I could pick her brain, if you will, and ask the questions that would give me better insight into who my mother was as a person. Not just as a mother, but as a woman.

I was privileged to be able to spend time with her in her final days in hospice. We would have wonderful conversations—mother to daughter, woman to woman, and mother to mother. I asked so many questions, and she answered them all with no hesitation, turning each one into a full conversation. Such wonderful stories that covered so many different aspects of her life.

My absolute favorite memory from Mom's time in hospice was watching her enjoy a glazed doughnut. It was in her final days, and taste was one of the last senses she still had at full strength. It was such a joy listening to her describe each and every bite while having the biggest smile on her face. She was giddy, like a child enjoying her first ever donut. She was absolutely beautiful in those moments.

The last time I went to Honduras was for her funeral. Though, it wasn't really a funeral. My siblings and I put together a Celebration of Life ceremony for her in Tela, and just about every single family member we had in Honduras attended. And we have a very, very large family. We were still receiving calls the morning of the ceremony informing us of other family members who were making the (for some) multi-hour drive to attend. We had the official Celebration of Life at a resort where all the out-of-town family were staying. A few days later, Aunt Ondina hosted a dinner in Elba's honor. So many aunts, uncles, and cousins, some whom I had not met before this trip, showed up. It was a real party, with a ridiculous amount of the best Honduran food. We drank, ate, and danced punta, salsa, merengue, and bachata late into the night. All in honor and celebration of my mother's life. Every picture from that night is full of smiles. Just like Mom would have wanted.

I inherited an impressive collection of wonderful traits from this exceptional woman. In fact, all of my memories of her are overwhelmingly positive. At least, they were. Then I started writing this book. A long buried memory came to light during one of my writing sessions—something I had suppressed so completely that I had not thought about it in decades.

Remember my stepfather, the much younger man my firecracker-of-a- mother married when I was young? They separated when I was twelve. I worked through the pain of that years ago. But I had forgotten that after the separation, my vibrant, vivacious, always capable mother didn't get out of bed for days. So neither did I.

Looking back, I can see that what my child eyes saw as the sadness of a woman in love was truly depression. Her grief went far beyond sadness—it was physical. She could not get out of bed. Perhaps my own depressive tendencies are another piece of my inheritance from her. At the very least, I mirrored her behavior. At twelve years old, I took on her depression, and also found myself too overcome with sorrow to leave my own bed.

A few days after the separation, my stepfather came back to pick up some of his things, and he and my mom started up a private conversation in their room. They had been talking for a while when the phone rang—it was one of my sisters calling, asking me to let our mother know she would get home late that night. She said it was important that I tell her as soon as I could.

I knocked on the bedroom door. Once mom acknowledged me, I opened it slightly, only sticking my head inside. I gave her the message and shut the door behind me. My stepfather left soon after, and my mother became deeply upset.

She questioned why I had knocked. Apparently, the conversation had been going well prior to my interruption. My message had broken the flow, and they had begun to argue again. She was short with me, demanding to know why I hadn't waited to deliver the message. Why I had ruined everything. I don't believe she said those words, but that is what I heard.

She retreated back to bed, and because of my guilt, I did the same. Our bedrooms were across from each other, and for days we both lay in bed with our bedroom doors shut, grappling with our own sadness.

This memory is hard for me to write about. What I once saw as a minor childhood slight I've come to understand was actually a traumatic experience. That was not easy for me to grasp because I have nothing but love and admiration for my mother. Still, I know that to heal, I must honor the truth of that moment. My mother, the loving and protective person she was, would want me to.

When this memory came to the forefront, it hit me hard. I dropped to my knees. The emotional weight from that childhood moment—guilt, shame, embarrassment, and hurt—surged back into my body. The mental and emotional affect is exhausting! As a child, I internalized blame for my stepfather leaving that day. I was overcome with guilt for how my actions affected my mother. His leaving shattered her heart and sent her into a deep depression, which in turn led me into my own.

This childhood trauma has been buried within me for over forty five years, without my knowing.

I am my mother's daughter. The apple didn't fall far from the tree. As a woman, I deeply empathize with my mother and the profound heartbreak she endured.

Yet I am also my children's mother. As a mother and "Mina" (a grandmother), my goal is to guide my family with emotional intelligence. I aspire for my children to surpass my achievements and for my granddaughter's generation to build upon their success. I understand, from the depths of my heart, that my mother never intended to cause me harm. This realization is the most comforting and heartwarming insight I've experienced throughout my healing journey. And I trust this book and my EIF will provide you with the same comfort on your own healing journey.

Do you have a childhood memory that you would consider unpleasant? I don't want you to misunderstand—I had a great childhood, but I also experienced trauma. Both can coexist. Give yourself the space and grace; the permission to look at your childhood memories. If necessary, acknowledge them, take the time to fully look at them. Then…Let. It. Go. Healing is possible.

Maybe I did inherit my depression from my mother. Regardless, I know for sure that I got my tenacity, my Honduran spirit, my beauty and class, and my lust for life from her too. I can only hope to leave such a vibrant legacy for my children, depression and all.

Throughout my life, Mom shared a handful of proverbs with me. "A drunk man always speaks the truth." "One bad apple will spoil the whole bunch." That one usually came out when I started spending time with a friend she didn't like. "Beware of the shy ones." She usually said that one with a smirk. And my absolute favorite, the one she would say with a wink in my direction no matter who else was in the room: "The best things come in small packages." That one was for me.

From the day she saw my shining spirit as I strutted in my Mary Janes, to the day she trusted me with that ridiculous machete, to all the ways she supported me throughout my life, big and small—my mother thought I could do anything. She never forgot my true self, the *fuego* within me. Even when I did.

When I left Roger, I knew I had work to do. I had lost sight of the little girl I had loved being. Revisiting my past and remembering the woman who made me was the beginning. If she could run a school at seventeen, move to a new country without speaking the language, raise six children on her own, and never lose her spark, maybe I could find that spark in me, too.

I got it from her, after all.

CHAPTER 10

Space and Grace

Did you know that the rate of depression among adolescents has been rising in the United States? It is estimated that there are 4.1 million adolescents ages twelve to seventeen in the United States who have had at least one depressive episode. That's almost one in every ten teens! 4.6% of adults ages eighteen and older are living with regular depression. Around 39% of adults with major depressive episodes do not receive treatment.

Major depression is described as experiencing at least two weeks of a depressed mood or loss of interest or pleasure in daily activities and exhibits several of a set of specific symptoms including problems with sleep, eating, energy, concentration, and self-worth.

And sadly, I am one of those adults. I know depression intimately; it's been a constant in my life. I have had a tumultuous relationship with depression for years, taking medications for both depression and sleep for fifteen consecutive years. Even with all of the global travel and the exterior appearance of a perfect life, I suffered. I've faced incredible setbacks and losses, some of which I didn't even recognize until I did. However, the gift of self-healing that my Emotional Intelligence Formula has provided continues to be truly life-changing.

My mother raised me to believe that if you don't have anything nice to say about someone, you don't say anything at all. With a house full of kids, mostly girls, who fought over clothes and boys and space and attention, it was a necessary lesson. My older sisters were close enough in age that, at times, they were interested in the same boys, and she didn't want them turning to gossip or cutting each other down. I, however, heard a different lesson. While my mom said, "Don't say anything mean," I heard, "Don't say anything."

You've seen me ignore my intuition again and again throughout this book. I spent years not expressing my needs or calling people out for the way they treated me. I knew deep down that the way Howard treated me was wrong, but I didn't want to rock the boat. I saw the hints that Roger wasn't listening to or seeing me, but I didn't want to call out his faults.

If you don't have anything nice to say, don't say anything at all.

For me, the depression, the anxiety, the sleepless nights, and the medication I needed just to engage with my life and sleep at the end of the day all stemmed from repression. Remember that day in Paris when I finally realized that the life around me was not the life I was meant to live? That started long ago, in my mother's kitchen, taking the wrong lesson from the right advice. I became someone who let a lot of water roll off her back without complaint, and I thought I was proud of it.

After my second marriage ended, I was single and living in Newport Beach, California. Then, COVID hit.

Newport Beach never really shut down, but everything changed all the same. My friendships started turning toxic, and my friends kept leaving.

Even my friendships with some of my sisters suffered during this time. I started rounding my edges trying to fit in, but that doesn't work. It became incredibly exhausting having conflict after conflict. In some of these friendships, lies were told about me: about my character, my morals, and my integrity. For years, my name was spoken about badly.

In one of these situations, a person whom I considered to be a good friend at the time accused me of stealing makeup, money, and a gift card (I think—it's been a while) from her purse. We had been out at a bar (remember, Newport Beach businesses stayed open through the pandemic). The bar we had been to that night had cameras, and the owner claimed to have video footage of the supposed theft. Unfortunately, I was never able to see the video. I asked her to show it to me, but she refused. I asked the owner to show it to me, but he couldn't because he had given the only copy to her. I was told by the owner that the video showed me in the proximity of her purse sometime before it was taken. That's it! That's all the video showed! Of course, I was close to her purse several times throughout the evening, as she was to mine. We were always together! She chose to spread the lies that I had stolen from her. She chose to keep this story up for two years. I can only assume that she wanted to take me down a peg. The lies that were said about me were beyond ridiculous, but they started to affect my relationships.

Let me state clearly: I did NOT steal any of the items that were taken from this person that night. Nor did I steal any of the other made up items she started lying about months after. And she knew that.

Even in the face of these lies, not once did I speak badly about her and her friends. Not one word. And I could have—I know truths about these people that would have made others look at them differently. But that's not who I am. Social outings started to feel like sitting with the mean girls at the lunch table, and still I said nothing. Again, if you don't have anything nice to say, don't say anything at all. And again, I patted myself on the back for being above it all.

The COVID pandemic continued.

I had so much loss in my life during this time. Loss of people I cared about due to COVID. Loss of friendships. Loss of appetite. Loss of sleep. Loss of self-esteem. Loss of identity.

Those friendships that I had tried so hard to repair finally ended. I lost them too.

In the madness that was COVID with all its uncertainties, I made the decision that I was fed up with pouring into relationships that would only bring criticism, negative energy, and upheaval to my life.

So, I stopped. Literally. I stopped socializing completely during the pandemic. I sat in my apartment with my dog, Gracie, for eight solid months. Alone.

I did not leave my apartment. I had very little interaction with anyone. Even my groceries came with contactless delivery. This experience was the norm in some parts of the world, but not here in Orange County, California. There was not much quarantining going on here. Life continued on as if COVID did not exist and, to some extent, for people in Orange County, life was lived as if COVID had not just shown up and overturned our lives.

For me, solitude was an *intentional* choice, one very much against the grain of Orange County society at the time. I wanted a hard reset.

In that solitude, I questioned everything about myself—my thoughts, emotions, behaviors, attitude, fears, and more.

I did a lot of soul-searching. I spent a lot of time digging deep into figuring out what was it within me that was contributing to the lack in these relationships. Have you ever done that? Dug so deep you faced the ugliness, the selfishness, all the harmful attributes that are a part of who you are, who you have become? I did. It was not pretty.

It was dark.

It was hard.

It was ugly.

It was painful.

It was necessary.

It was gut-wrenching at times to come to understand parts of myself that I did not like. For a while, I had felt subconsciously that I did not like myself. Now those feelings were in full view. And why.

It was a tough process, recognizing myself for exactly who I had been and changing into someone I wanted to be. It took a lot of discipline and self-love, and did not happen overnight. But I am nothing if not tenacious. I stuck with it.

I cut a lot of people, places, and things out of my life. It happened naturally for me. And my energy changed. My mentality changed. I changed. And definitely for the better. As I sit and write this, it's been almost four solid years of consistency in what I now look back on as my transformational time. And dare I say that I love the transformations that have happened for me. I not only like me; I love me. It has been a long time since I've felt that way. It feels amazing, rewarding, and downright fantastic!

I now believe that not liking myself, not fully understanding why I did not like myself, and a lack of self, accompanied by my anxiety, and a dash of depression thrown in all played a significant role in the process of losing myself in my marriage to Roger. All those times I sat on the sofa with my depression, feeling anxious, feeling like I was meant for more but not knowing what that was. For so many years I couldn't put my finger on it. Little did I know then that the "more" I was looking for was within me the whole time, waiting for me to take the time to search within myself to find it. To find me.

I found myself in solitude. This time of transformation was when I first started to create a formula that worked for me. It continues to work for me because, as I mentioned, it's a process. I still don't know what I wanna be when I grow up. Do you? Are you who you imagined you would be at this point in your life? I am not referring to a career or anything status-related, I am asking you: Are you the quality of person you imagined yourself to be at this age, when you were a child? I am not quite there yet, but man! I am a lot closer to being that person than I was a few years ago. And the journey has brought so much peace and joy into my life! The best part of it all... No one can ever take that peace or joy away from me because I have consistently worked on healing myself from hurt, pain, trauma, triggers, etc. I have done that for myself, by myself. No one can ever take it away. It's the greatest gift I could have ever given to myself. Is there a greater gift that you could give yourself? Are you willing to take the necessary steps to a better version of you, a happier version of you?

As I have mentioned, shadow work is a practice that I have done several times now, for several years. And it will continue being an ongoing practice of self-evaluation, a mindset of continuing to move forward, a periodic, energetic check-in with myself, a change of aspects of myself that I do not like, and, most importantly, self-love. Plenty of space, grace, and self-love.

I took the time to examine every situation I had found myself in over the past few months. Every failed or toxic friendship. And I noticed a pattern.

I have heard it said that people come into our lives for a reason, a season, or a lifetime. I thought these particular friendships were only meant for a season. They ended, and that was that. But I was wrong. They were in my life for a reason. There was a lesson here that I was refusing to learn. My friendships and relationships would keep ending until I learned the lesson.

I remember THE moment the thought occurred to me, because it came to me with a mental picture and a musical lyric. I'm a very visual person, and I've been a fan of several genres of music all my life—as well as taking the opportunity to dance every chance I get. The lyric I heard was Sesame Street's "One of These Things Is Not Like the Others," with the mental picture of the four boxes within a box—with three similar pictures and one different from the rest. That was me. I was the one different from the rest. But I hadn't been allowing myself to be my authentic self. I hadn't been honest about my needs and wants, and I had let these friends say whatever they wanted about me and to me in the pursuit of being nice. They didn't step on me and round my edges—*I* let them do that. It was me all along.

When I didn't have anything nice to say, I said nothing. When I learned something unsavory about a friend, I said nothing. I was proud of that. But when someone mistreated me, I also said nothing. I didn't say anything about the way I was being treated.

Somehow, my mom's beautiful lesson had morphed in my brain. She never wanted me to dull my light or accept this kind of treatment. How could she? She was full of light, that beautiful tenacious spirit that I am so proud to have inherited from her. She wouldn't want to silence me. She just wanted peace among her daughters.

I wanted to fit in with local individuals, rounding my edges, making myself small so that others could feel better about themselves. That was a mistake! A complete waste of time and a complete disservice to myself. Not to mention the time, energy and effort it takes to do so is not worth it.

I was investing my time, my energy, and my emotions into relationships that did not serve me, only to be torn down mentally, emotionally, and at times financially.

I had had it, I was done! No more! It was time to take full accountability and learn how to foster better friendships.

COVID was a gift to me. Self-inflicted solitude was a gift to me.

Not only has this process taught me a lot about myself, it also taught me a lot about those I had considered to be friends. Which is, not everyone has the same good intentions as you. Not everyone is happy to see you succeed. And I have every right to cut those people out of my life, even to be honest about how they treated me. How dare I!

Now I dare. The lessons are learned, the standards are raised, and the friendships in my life today will last a lifetime. We have the same interests, mindset, morals, integrity, love, and support for one another. We continue to uplift each other through life's trials and tribulations as well as many wonderful celebrations. That is what real friendships are all about!

Just like "true love" affects a relationship positively, so does "true" friendship. The relationships become more enriching, loving, and supportive. A true friendship affects you differently, it affects your world differently.

And when I found self-love and my friendships turned around, I received another incredible surprise gift. I was able to stop taking the antidepressants and sleep medication my body had needed to function.

After you have suppressed so many traumas for years, your body and your mindset will begin to crave the low frequency that is associated with hurt, pain, disillusions, etc. I was medicating the symptoms of that low energy, but I wasn't doing anything to raise the frequency. I had to admit I was addicted to trauma and had to take control and accountability of my mindset. That was the only way to stop sabotaging myself with negative, fear-based thoughts that would keep pulling me back into those feelings.

The only reason that I was successful without the medications, and continue to be successful, is by spending so much time by myself—self-evaluating and continuously reevaluating my life. For a lack of a better way of putting it, it was by doing shadow work.

For me, as I said to Roger that afternoon in Paris, I already knew I didn't like myself. I had known that about me for a while. And as shadow work tends to do, it made me face the conscious and unconscious aspects of my personality, character, attitude, and temperament that I did not like. It's a continuous work ethic or investment in myself. Or, as I choose to see it now, it is part of my self-love.

Because of the three years of shadow work that I had done at this point in my life, my Emotional Intelligence Formula evolved organically. The EIF became a natural process for me. Each step individually came to me in the moment that I needed it. It took time. The more time I spent on shadow work—which brought so many great things into my life, into my psyche—-the more spiritual I became and I continue to become. And the more in tune I became with my intuition, and so many other aspects of myself that I love.

With time, consistency, lots of self-love, space and grace, self-appreciation, and boundaries—lots of boundaries—my formula became a four-step process that I continue to practice. My formula has been a lifesaver for me. It has kept me sane, released me from my medications, and pushed me to become the most authentic version of myself for the first time in years. I found myself. Winner, winner—chicken dinner! That's a major accomplishment! Don't you agree?

In reading my book, you have witnessed my journey through depression. That journey has existed in five stages. I refer to them as my Five Stages of Expansion.

The first stage is Situational. It is the stage that initiated the start of my transformation through shadow work. My spirituality was beginning to flutter within me in certain situations that, unbeknownst to me, were triggered from trauma.

The second stage is Biological. I would mentally, emotionally, and physically realign, sometimes several times a day. Our bodies get physically and mentally addicted to negative and/or positive thoughts, and emotions. There were times I would feel sad, and when I would sit in my energy and analyze it, I couldn't find a reason. My body had become addicted to my stress responses. I had to learn how to calm my nervous system before I could heal. Give yourself the space and grace to listen to your body and give it what it needs: breath, rest, food, a hug, etc.

The third stage is Psychological. Readjusting my mindset to change certain pieces of myself I did not like and wanted to improve upon. No longer taking medications meant learning to actually deal with issues and situations that continued to occur during writing the book. Learning a new mindset and unlearning old habits.

The fourth stage is Existential. By repeating my Emotional Intelligence Formula, I have been able to achieve the inner knowing and understanding that I am becoming who I was meant to be.

The fifth stage is Spiritual. Being open to connecting with myself on a deeper level in the hopes of getting to know who the hell I am and leaning into my intuition was THE reason that spirituality has been a common thread through all of my self-evaluating, self-worth, self-love, and self-healing.

My mindset coach says that if you keep in alignment with your vision, you will receive what you want "or something better." This fifth stage of expansion was my "something better." In working my formula and processing my repressed trauma, I have accessed a surprise spiritual strength that gives my life the meaning I had been looking for. I have gotten a lot of "something better" lately.

In the last couple of years, I have learned that actively practicing listening to my intuition has enabled me to live my "more"! I have learned that I have to trust my intuition. I have to trust myself. I have to trust that what is meant for me is already mine. What is meant for me is all coming to me in perfect timing. It has been long and difficult, but one of the most rewarding journeys of my life. I know that in continuing to live by my Emotional Intelligence Formula I am living my purpose. I am living my Meant for More!

And. You. Will. Too.

Letter to My Reader from Me

My Dearest Reader,

I hope that reading my book impacts you like it impacted me in the process of writing it. It has helped me heal parts of myself that I had been repressing for far too long. In reading my book, you held my hand through the process of my personal journey of shadow work, self-healing, self-evaluating, accountability, and spirituality.

Now it's my turn. Let me hold your hand as you make your way into the life that is meant for you. You are also not alone in your journey; I am here for you. My Emotional Intelligence Formula is here for you. My book, Meant for More, is here for you. We will walk with you on the path to your healing, your emotional expansion, and your spirituality—if you choose to do so. Let my book and my Emotional Intelligence Formula hold your hand during your healing journey. Give yourself the gifts of Self-Love, Self-Worth, Peace, Joy, and Happiness.

Putting pen to paper in writing about and acknowledging my life has been extremely rewarding as well as extremely painful at times. There are a few chapters in my book that cut to the raw matter of...pain. With the words on paper in front of me, I had no choice but to acknowledge who I had become in the process of repressing trauma for so long. I had no choice but to acknowledge who I am today after acknowledging, taking accountability, and healing traumas. The growth, self-worth, and self-love undeniably come with that hard work.

I urge you, my friend: Give yourself THE greatest gift of all. Give yourself the gifts of self-love, self-worth, joy, peace, and happiness by healing your repressed or suppressed trauma. I ask you, what greater gift can you give yourself?

I see you. I appreciate you. I love you.

Now, let's move from…Let. It. Go. to Let's Go!!!

Your friend,
Elba Raquel

CHAPTER 11

In God I Trust

After my year of solitude, I felt ready to go out again, to socialize, to put my newfound confidence and coping skills into practice. Even ready to finally set and enforce boundaries in my life. It was time for new friends and a new beginning. And, right away, these skills were tested.

One evening, I went to play pool at my favorite hole-in-the-wall bar on the Balboa Peninsula. This particular game was quite competitive, with both teams knowing the game inside out. At one point, I was left with only one shot—one that required me to straddle the table to make it. Let me preface this by saying that I'm short. While I'm full of fire, I'm not exactly tall. That's probably why I feel more at ease in heels, especially when playing pool. Heels come in handy when you need to lift one leg over the table, lean forward, and aim. It's not my favorite maneuver, but I do it when necessary. I glanced at my partner, who immediately understood my dilemma. He shrugged as if to say, "Hey, it's the only shot you got."

So I did. I straddled the table to take my shot. As I lined it up, a disgusting embarrassment of a male specimen standing in my line of vision made a full-on sexual gesture with his entire body towards me.

Of course, I missed the shot.

I had seen this man, Mike, there several times before. I had even shot pool with him a few times in the past at this same establishment. I should also mention that at some point at the beginning of this particular summer he had asked me out. I was not interested in him at all. I had let him know that I saw him only as a friend and I was not interested in dating. I don't remember if this was my first time seeing him since that conversation took place.

After I straightened up, he walked over to me, and I asked him, "Why? Why did you do that? You're not even involved in this game."

His response was horrifying. "Because. I. Can. Just know anytime you straddle the table, to me it's going to be a sexual thing."

Gross! Who in their right mind talks like that?! You know who? A predator, that's who! And I truly believe in my heart that it is not the only time he has preyed on a female. I believe I was just one of many.

As the evening progressed, Mike's behavior became even more predatory. He wasn't getting the rouse out of me that I suspect he wanted, so he became relentless. Several times throughout the night he tried approaching me with very derogatory and explicitly sexual comments, but he wasn't able to "break me," if you will. His behavior was actually prompting me to ignore him instead of confront him like he seemed to want. The lack of attention was not sitting well with him.

At the end of the night, I was sitting in the back of the bar on one of the bench seats by the ladies' room. Mike approached me and offered his hand to shake as a "good game" gesture. I looked down at his hand, sat further back in my seat, and shook my head "no."

Mike proceeded to pop my face—somewhere between a slap and a push; with his open palm. It was a hard, shocking blow. What an ass! I called the police and filed a report, which led to a case number and eventually assigned a detective. Taking this step felt empowering, as it was a significant act of standing up for myself. Although I had been advocating for myself for years, this was a new level of self-assertion.

I don't want to get into any more detail about this situation, because I have put it behind me. I have let it go. I want you to know that nothing came of it except my own growth.

Needless to say, this brought on another round of shadow work for me. I spent days, weeks, alone, allowing myself to sit in the silence of solitude and to feel all the emotions that this violent act created within me. It was a dark time. It was neither fun nor easy. It was definitely necessary for me to work through the emotions, to identify them, to label them. During that process I cried a lot. I got angry.

But amidst that anger a sense of pride grew. I had stood up for myself, filed against an abusive man—something I never did with Howard. The first step of drawing the line in the sand, if you will, was to fully stand up for myself, which was transformative for me. After the first time, it becomes completely natural to do so moving forward in life. It's made living life by my standards, my boundaries, and not anyone else's a lot more peaceful, enjoyable, and joyful! Who would have thought?! Surely not me.

That asshole was not relevant in my life and could not take anything away from me. I put him behind me. I Let. It. Go. And despite my previous patterns, I started to consistently maintain peace in my life. Wow, real growth!

I hadn't always been so evolved. Three years earlier, I let a "friend" upset my peace to the point where I had to move to regain it. This friend was on her way to an international trip and made a pit stop in California to hang out with me for a few days. She stayed in my apartment for those days…and then a few more…and then this stay turned into eight months. She paid me once, an amount that was not a third of a single month's rent. When I returned from Ashley and Steve's wedding, I met someone at the complex's Jacuzzi who asked which unit was mine. When I pointed out the unit, they said, "Oh, that's [my friend]'s apartment." She had been hosting people in my apartment while I was gone, as if it was hers! Eventually, on one of our nights out a few days before Christmas, one of our conversations turned violent. I told her to get out, but the woman wouldn't leave. She. Would. Not. Leave.

The lease was in my name. Actually, everything was in my name. So, I ended my lease and transferred to another apartment in the same complex. I had to leave my home to be free of her.

Three years later, I had learned some things. I did not let Mike take away my peace. But unfortunately, my shiny new backbone wasn't enough to keep me in Newport. I had to move again—this time for my own safety. My Ring camera captured audio and video of people I didn't know stalking my apartment. Among them were a handful of faces I recognized, women who had been part of my social circle at the pool club. I had no idea why they would stalk my place. This continued for weeks. It was clear in their body language, tone, and conversations that these people did not have good intentions.

I have no idea why any of these individuals felt the need to take these actions toward me. I mind my own business. I have enough on my own plate without having to deal with anyone else's drama. Since a few of them were regulars at the pool club, I wondered if they knew Mike. Was he the cause of this harassment? I honestly don't know.

This time I did not try to fix my friendships at the pool club. I did not round my edges to fit into this community that supported Mike. Those recordings on my Ring camera were like a blaring siren telling me to get out now. God was telling me these were not my people.

So I left. I moved away. Who has the time for drama? I would rather continue to put my time, focus, and energy into myself and my life. That is a direct result of working my EIF. I was already a different person from the old me. I was having conversations about ideas for my book, my mindset, my future plans. I was not interested in the drama.

I had made plans to move out of California anyway. My ducks were all in a row—my lease was ending soon, I had made arrangements to move in with a sister in Louisiana, and I was ready for a fresh start. So the move itself was not a surprise. But the way the move happened certainly was. Here I was, moving out of my *home* because of malicious actions of others who intended to do me harm…again. Heart-wrenching! Every bit of control was taken out of my hands when it came to that move, almost like I was back in Philly running from Howard all over again. Can you imagine?

Despite my sorrow at once again fleeing my home in a hurry, I couldn't ignore the signs. This is not where I was meant to be at this stage of my life. These will never be my people. God plucked all the ducks that I had so meticulously put in place and kicked them out of the way. These were not even my ducks!

I had honed my intuition enough to heed the red flags. And boy, there were plenty in this phase of my life. But expanding my emotional intelligence also helped me see the green flags, the beautiful ways that God has always provided support along the way. Despite the ups and downs of so many of my friendships, I have been blessed with some truly beautiful people in my life. I have had safe havens amidst the chaos.

Two come to mind immediately: Brad and Mark. They're best friends. Mark was kind enough when I first moved to Newport Beach to introduce me around, which made it easier to meet people originally. As time went on Mark became like a brother to me. He and his daughter Kelsea have always been dear to me. When I entered my self-imposed sabbatical from life during COVID, we grew distant. However, I would run into Mark every now and again, and we always pick up right where we left off. Mark will forever be my brother from another mother!

Brad and I met shortly before I moved to Orange County. He became a very important person to me in the sense that he was the only consistent person in my life who was always reaching out and getting in touch with me to check how things were going. When we first met, we dated for a few months, and it was great fun!

Brad is kind, he has a wicked sense of humor, and we all know how important a great sense of humor is to me. Without even trying, he has always had a way about him that makes me feel at home in his presence. We are very competitive in fun ways and spend time together playing games. During these times he always talks so much shit. And I love it! He could back up all the trash talk he'd been spewing, and it was always in a playful, fun manner. Especially over a game of pool!

Looking back, Brad was the one constant during my bouts of solitude. He was there for me through so much loss. We were there for each other. His staying in touch has meant the world to me.

CHAPTER 12

A New Legacy

When we lived in Sun City, South Africa, it wasn't uncommon to learn—almost daily—about someone who found a snake, a spider, or a scorpion in their home. Typically in the shower, in closets, in shoes, etc. Almost as frequent were whispers of pets that went missing, probably taken by a wild monkey or large cat. The accommodations were lovely, but they were recently constructed on land that had long been occupied by wild animals. It was their home first.

One day I was lying in the yard enjoying the beautiful sunny afternoon with a few friends and their little ones around me when I heard one of the young girls screaming Elijah's name. In all the chaos, only three words cut through:

Elijah…baboon…Cheetos. I ran!

I immediately ran toward the area she had come from. I hurdled over my friend's daughter's head on my way through the back door of our townhome. As soon as I stepped out the front door, I saw Elijah running down the hill toward me, screaming, tears streaming down his little red face. He was hysterically clutching a bag of Cheetos as if his little life depended on it!

And evidently, it did! One of the larger male baboons was hungry and brave enough to make his way down to where the kids were all playing together. At one point, Elijah looked up to see a baboon in his personal space! The baboon tried snatching the bag of Cheetos out of Elijah's hands, but Elijah was not having it. He clutched those Cheetos with a tenacity he definitely got from his mother and ran off screaming. As it was retold to me, the kids around were not sure who was the loudest, Elijah or the baboon!

The heavens were looking down on Elijah that day. The fact that he was able to get away from the baboon, Cheetos in hand, was a blessing! Luckily, other than Elijah's pride, he wasn't hurt. All I could do when I saw my little boy crying with his bag of Cheetos clenched tightly in his little hand was to pick him up, kiss his little face, and give him plenty of tight hugs. My son stood up to a full-grown baboon and lived to tell the story. Elijah told me recently that he has not eaten Cheetos since! He does remember his immediate thought once he saw the baboon up close. It was to run. Run! So he did. What a lasting impression from a childhood experience. The incident with the baboon made an impression on Elijah to last a lifetime.

What his little nervous system was experiencing in those moments, I can't even imagine. Elijah was four or five years old when this happened. For him to have had the wherewithal to comprehend the extent of the situation he was in, to run for his own protection, is completely mind-boggling to me.

How he didn't stand there and freeze in the moment of such terror is incomprehensible to me! The courage, determination, and tenacity Elijah needed to have within himself at such a young age to refuse to release *his* bag of Cheetos to a big, scary baboon…that was inherited from his momma!

My son inherited from me the same tenacity that I held onto with such determination when I was that little four-pound, three-ounce baby who looked like a brown frog being carried around on a pillow by my mother. Thank God Elijah inherited my tenacity. It definitely made all the difference that scary day in South Africa.

It is wonderful to know that an inclination for depression is not the only aspect of me that my children will inherit. My tenacity, determination, courage, strength, and yes, even my sense of humor are inherited too!

Later in life, Elijah and I went through some really challenging times together.

When he was seven years old, I found a letter that he had handwritten in his little-boy handwriting that was folded neatly and tucked underneath his pillow. My blood ran cold reading it.

He wrote that he felt he had nothing to live for, that he had no joy in his life. He was incredibly unhappy. So unhappy, in fact, that he had already chosen the knife in our kitchen that he would use to end his life. He had even drawn a picture of the knife with blood dripping from it. My throat closes just at the thought of it.

I called Elijah into his room, sat on his bed next to him, and showed him the note I had found. He had no reaction. None.

He spoke to me in a matter-of-fact tone. His demeanor made me feel like I was speaking to a grown man, not to my seven-year-old son. How could I not have seen this? How could I, his mother, not know how my son was experiencing life? I love my son. I adore him. How could I not have known? I cannot find the words to describe how I felt. There are no words. Only pain.

The incredible guilt that followed, and stayed with me for so many years, was palpable within me. I cry as I write this because I am still baffled by that note. I carried guilt around with me for a very long time. I showed the note to Roger, and I went over my conversation with Elijah. Roger then, too, went upstairs to speak with Elijah.

After a short time, he came downstairs and took control of the situation. He immediately called our insurance company who referred us to the best child psychiatrist in our area. By 10 o'clock the next morning, we were sitting in her office: Elijah, Roger, and I.

Elijah ended up getting diagnosed with ADHD at age seven and a mild form of bipolar disorder at fourteen. Elijah saw a psychiatrist and a psychologist from the age of seven until he was seventeen. And I was right there with him.

I had promised myself as a teenager that I would have my children while I was still young, so I could truly understand and relate to their experiences. I'm incredibly grateful I kept that promise, especially given everything Elijah faced during his teenage years. For many years raising Elijah became a constant mind game, and an emotional tug-of-war within myself, trying to analyze and figure out his behavior. Luckily, I had an advantage. It was a blessing in disguise to have so much in common with my son.

During Elijah's teenage years, his mindset and behavior became increasingly challenging, both at home and at school. It was often difficult to determine whether his actions were just typical teenage behavior or signs of a deeper issue. I had to navigate this fine line carefully, balancing my approach between letting him work through common adolescent struggles and intervening when necessary.

To manage the situation, I implemented a system that took into account his therapy, tools, medications, and lifestyle. This system helped differentiate between normal teenage behavior and symptoms related to his diagnosis and medication side effects. It was often said that living with a teenager felt like dealing with someone who had swapped heads while keeping the same body. For me, this analogy meant amplifying the usual teenage challenges by tenfold and scrutinizing each situation through various lenses: whether it was typical teenage behavior, a side effect of medication, or a mix of both.

In addition to these considerations, I had to think about his grades, social circles, and friendships, all while adhering to the principle of "It is not my mistake to make." Managing these aspects was overwhelming at times, but it was crucial for navigating the complexities of his teenage years.

When Elijah was first diagnosed with ADHD, he was prescribed medication he had to take during the school day. All the relevant adults were notified. At one point, I received a phone call from the school nurse informing me that Elijah had not come to her for his meds in two weeks. I was confused. He had not missed a day of school in weeks. Why had he not gone to the nurse?

I spoke with his teacher only to be told by her that she had not been sending him to the nurse's station. In her opinion, ADHD did not exist. Excuse me?! I very clearly informed her that when it comes to my son's health, she did not have an opinion. Her only job and responsibility for my son, while he was in her class, was his education!

I marched straight to the principal's office, insisted on speaking with her without an appointment, informed her what had been taking place, and insisted that Elijah be transferred to another class. I told her to educate herself and the school teachers on what children and their families go through with ADHD to understand how important it is to have each day match the day before, especially with their medication. Elijah was moved to another class, and I chose not to inform his teacher why she had to send him to the nurse once a day. It was my decision to make and I made it.

Eventually, I started noticing a difference in Elijah. He became more aware of his symptoms, his moods, and how the medications made him feel. Getting the perfect dosage for Elijah was a crucial element in the process. He made it easy by letting me know how each change in dose affected his mindset, energy level, behavior, and such.

With the help of therapy from his psychologist and psychiatrist, and aided by medication, love, patience, discipline, and understanding (difficult at times), Elijah grew out of his mild form of bipolar and his behavioral disorders.

As you know, "not my mistake to make" had been part of my parental mindset, so I expanded on that with all "your choices have consequences." Tough love was necessary at times.

At one point, when Elijah was a teenager, he got into trouble at school. It was a challenging time with Elijah, and I had been implementing harsher consequences to deal with his choices. In this situation, we took the extreme stance of removing almost everything from his room. The only things left were his "necessities" to get through the day—his bed, night stand, lamp, clothes, shoes, book bag, and school supplies. Roger took his bedroom door off its hinges. Elijah had no privacy whatsoever! He was confined to his bedroom, and he had to earn everything back that had been in his room. We stored his belongings in the laundry room under lock and key.

What I remember about this punishment is how Elijah handled it. Of course, he wasn't happy, but knew he had brought these consequences on himself. At the end of every week we reviewed his assignments, homework, and test scores, in addition to his behavior at home and school. Every week he earned something back. There was a system as to what and how many items he could earn back. Elijah earned every piece of each game, every single toy, every figurine, every TV, stereo, toy car remote, Game Boy, stereo, etc. It took time. But he did it! And he was always very proud of himself when he did. He still talks about this particular punishment to this day. It made a lifetime impression on him.

That particular punishment for Elijah is similar to how I see my shadow work. You peel away the layers of onion that is you—just as we peeled back the onion of Elijah's room, which is an extension of him, and left it bare. It forced Elijah to acknowledge the choices he had made to get him to the consequences he was left to deal with. In the process of shadow work you become vulnerable, you bare yourself in order to acknowledge what needs to change, what needs to be improved on, and the aspects of you that need to be let go.

As wonderful as it was that my son was now getting the therapy he needed, it also brought out what I believed to be my shortcomings as a mother. The weight of guilt I carried around with me for so many years was an incredibly heavy weight to carry, even as he was getting the therapy and tools he needed to succeed. I remember stating this to his psychologist, that I felt responsible for what he was going through. I still feel like I missed something along the way that was important for me to catch. I will never forget the moment the psychologist put his hand on my shoulder, looked me in the eyes, and said, "All you can do is make what you consider to be the best decision in any given moment." There are no words to describe the comfort he gave me by saying this. Unbeknownst to me, these feelings of inadequacy as a mother are what led to my depression. One afternoon, sitting in Elijah's psychiatrist office towards the end of the appointment, he leaned in and told me that he thought I was depressed and that I should seek therapy. Ha! Can you imagine?!

Unfortunately, he was not wrong. I was diagnosed shortly after. Sadly for me, my journey with depression began.

Fast forward to today. Elijah is a grown man, and he is a good man. He's a good person with a good heart. He has a great sense of humor! He's a man who works hard, loves hard, and likes to enjoy life with those he loves.

As adults, Elijah and I have traveled along parallel lines, especially in the last few years. The insights that I have gained through all my shadow work, creating my Emotional Intelligence Formula, and working with my mindset coach, I have shared with Elijah. He considers me his life coach—his words, not mine.

It is interesting looking back on the time when Elijah was younger, during the most vulnerable times of his life while dealing with ADHD and all that comes with it, that I didn't have the knowledge, skills, and experience with depression that I have now. I had not begun my personal journey with depression and shadow work—nor had I developed my EIF. Life for both of us would have looked a lot different.

Experiencing Elijah's ADHD alongside him—attending therapy with both his psychologist and his psychiatrist, managing his medication, learning how to help him get through school and prepare for life—has benefited me when it comes to my depression, shadow work, and the organic way my Emotional Intelligence Formula came to me. It is all due to my experience raising Elijah.

Unfortunately for my son, I did not have the knowledge, experience, or my EIF back then. But I have them now, and it is *never* too late to heal our traumas and discover our *fuego* within. Even as adults, Ashley and Elijah have benefited from my hard work and commitment to being the better version of myself. Ashley and Elijah will continue the new family legacy that I have started: authentic joy in life full of *fuego*. Plus, the family legacy doesn't end with them.

CHAPTER 13

Mia Is a Happy Girl!

Tiny fingers wrapped around my right index finger, gripping it tightly, as if saying, "Come on, Mina. Let's go!" It was the first time I met the most beautiful human being on earth—my granddaughter, Mia. I was lucky enough to capture that precious bonding moment in a photo, and I find myself looking at it often. Every time I do, my heart flutters like butterfly wings, warmth flows through my entire body—from the tips of my toes to the tingling at the top of my head—and I can't help but break into the biggest, most joyful smile. Every. Single. Time.

Mia is my special girl. How could she be anything less than perfect when she's the daughter of my lovely Ashley? She calls me "Mina," and let me tell you, Mia and Mina share an incredible bond. We have this little thing where we "boop" each other's nose with the tip of a finger, which always brings out smiles and laughter. We spend our time playing games, singing songs, and making green hearts out of Play-Doh. But nothing beats our dance parties—every Mina and Mia playdate turns into a dance-off! Baby girl's got rhythm, and like her Mina, she loves to dance! Mia is smart, kind, sweet, and incredibly perceptive for her age—not to mention beautiful inside and out, just like her momma.

Mia's presence has been a lifeline in my healing journey, a breath of fresh air I didn't even know I needed. She's been a source of pure love, making my transformation easier and so much more rewarding. Because of Mia, my cup truly runneth over. She's the cherry on my cake, the pep in my step, and a huge part of the fire that's been reignited within me.

The renewed energy, joy, and love she continues to give and bring into my life has been a life changing experience for me. Who knew the pure, innocent love of a child, a grandchild, could elevate your mindset and reinvigorate your life to such a degree? I did not. I welcome it. I embrace it. I love it. I look for it. And I will continue to nurture it for the rest of my life.

I have a way with Mia that is simply supernatural. I am teaching her to expand her emotional intelligence, and that little girl learns faster than any adult I know.

One gorgeous sunny day, Mia and I were sitting at the edge of the pool in Ashley and Steve's yard. Mia kept shoving my foot into the water, making splash after splash wash over us. When the water would hit her, she would laugh her delicious laugh that energizes every aspect of my being. I feel it viscerally throughout my body. That's the effect Mia has over me in general but especially when she laughs. The fact that it sounds so adorable is just a bonus!

It was a perfect moment.

At one point, Mia lost her balance. I caught her just as her outstretched arms dipped under the water. Immediately, tears.

I sat her on my lap. She leaned into me as she was crying. As I dried her with a towel, I spoke to her soothingly.

"The water is cold, Mia, but you are fine."

I continued drying her off in between cuddles and reassurances, sitting her up tall while I wiped away the tears on her face.

"See, you're not wet anymore. Mina dried you. Are you okay?"

She thought for a moment, then said, "Yes." Then, I asked the question I've been asking her since she was three months old.

"Mia, are you a Happy Girl?"

We've done this check-in together her whole life. When she gets upset, I ask her to think about what she is feeling. I ask her questions that make her self-evaluate.

Are you okay?

Are you hurt?

Are you wet?

Do you have to potty?

Are you hungry or thirsty?

Are you sad or mad?

The questions I ask bring her back to the present moment. She has to think about what she is feeling to answer me. Unless she has an "owie" or doesn't feel well, which we deal with immediately, Mia usually realizes that there's nothing wrong. There is no reason to cry.

Mind you, in the moments when she needs to express herself, she is given the space and grace to do so. There are moments that, like most toddlers, she does not want to speak to anyone and does not want anyone to speak to her. While Mia does not like to hear the word "no," she certainly loves to say it! I am sure every parent can relate to those toddler moments. Am I right? I can even remember some of Elijah and Ashley's toddler quirks.

In those moments, I give her space. I don't necessarily leave the room, but I pick up a book or my phone. Before I know it, when she's ready, Mia inevitably approaches me in some way. It doesn't take more than a few minutes.

My interactions with Mia when she has a breakdown are basically having her work the steps to my Emotional Intelligence Formula, but at the level of a two year old.

I always end with asking, "Are you a Happy Girl?" Most times, she replies with a "yes." If not, we talk about what's wrong and what will make her happy at that moment. Usually it is something simple, such as a cup of water, a hug, or putting her favorite show on the TV.

Teaching her to be in the moment, to acknowledge and feel her emotions in that moment, I feel, is a way to learn how to control her emotions. I don't think we can ever be too young to learn how to do that. Do you?

Back to sitting at the side of the pool. Mia took a moment before she responded. I could see her little wheels turning as she analyzed how she was feeling. Am I happy? The sun was shining, she was warm and dry, and we were playing together.

She was not falling in the water, she was not wet. She smiled and said, "Yes!"

I asked her for a hug and a kiss, which she gave me before running off to play with a happy giggle.

My goal with Mia is to teach her how to understand the feelings that come with different circumstances and conflicts, and how they may impact her in the moment. As a child, I was not taught how to identify or deal with emotions in conflict or in trauma situations. I was told, "Be a big girl. Get up, wipe your face, and keep it moving." Which is why, I believe, I suppressed my traumas. I kept it moving! That has clearly reared back and bitten me in the ass several times throughout my life. And, most times I was not even aware of it. Why? Because I suppressed that too.

I am convinced that, if I would have been taught how to identify and process my emotions, my life would have been different. For example, not once during my entire marriage to Howard did I acknowledge, identify, nurture, or question any emotion that I was experiencing, other than fear. The fear is what kept me moving, doing whatever I had to do to get the three of us out of the state of Pennsylvania unharmed. I suppressed every single other emotion that my body was going through. I suppressed them for well over thirty years until the day I started writing this book. Then all the emotions rose to the surface. I experienced the trauma all over again.

I do not want this for Mia. I believe it is avoidable. I believe in teaching Mia how to acknowledge her emotions. Why haven't we taught our children the roles that emotions play in all experiences in life from day one?

We teach them how to hold utensils so they can feed themselves, how to use scissors safely, how to crawl in order to learn how to walk. Why do we not teach our children how to sit in the emotion, how to identify it, and how to work through those emotions in difficult times?

As parents we all want the generations that come after us to live a better life than our own generation. To teach the young all we've learned to help them move further in life than we did. At least that's my goal.

The repression of trauma and emotions ends with me. It is not something that is going to be handed down to my children or my granddaughter's generation of my family. I have not gone through what I have been through, learned the lessons I have learned through pain, heartache, and repressed trauma, to then turn around and keep everything I have learned to myself. What a disservice that would be!

My formula is going to break generational traumas for me and my family. And it can be that for you and your family too! Do you have a generational trauma in your healing process, and journey, that you healed from? Did you teach those around you who are interested in healing by sharing your personal experiences as I have with you in *Meant for More*?

My Mia gets it! On our Mia & Mina days, Mia tells me a few times while we are together, as we play together, "Mina, I happy." The smiles on her face are endless and beautiful.

Mia is beginning to understand her emotions and the effect they have on her. I know this because she shows it in her behavior and her mindset. What could easily become a tantrum or an emotional breakdown becomes "Mina, I thirsty" or "Mina, I tired" or "Mina, I got an owie." She points to where it hurts, I kiss it and I ask, "Does that feel better?" Mia says, "Yes, better."

Mia communicates her emotions and experiences. The most beautiful effect of this is that Mia is *choosing* to be a Happy Girl throughout her day. We see it every day.

Mia and Mina days are not just about teaching or guiding Mia through emotions. We play, sing, and dance together. It is typically in these moments that Mia tells me she's happy, with a big cheesy smile on her face that lights up her entire face and makes her eyes twinkle. I can see the *fuego* that I had as a child shining through. In those moments I feel her joy and happiness viscerally.

Will you choose to do the work consistently by working the four steps to the Emotional Intelligence Formula that will lead you to live more of the life you are meant for? I am. I did. I still do. I am living my life every day to be the best version of me. I have found my *fuego*, and I will continue to share what I have learned with Mia so that we can both continue to be Happy Girls. I stand tall and proud in claiming that I will share and teach what I have learned to my granddaughter. I dare to love and nurture her emotional intelligence beyond what was nurtured in me.

It is my deepest desire that reading this book has helped you too. You will live every day as the best version of yourself. I hope this book helped you realize that *fuego*—that unique spark—is inside of you right now. And all you have to do to access it is to have the desire within yourself to change, to allow yourself to be vulnerable in facing all aspects of yourself in order for your desired changes to occur, to become comfortable in sitting in silence in your own energy. And finally…acknowledge, accept, and let go of all negative thoughts, narratives that you have allowed either yourself or others to think about you that do not align with who you authentically are. Your "something better" will be the ability to let go and move forward being your authentic self living the life that has always been meant for you.

Letter to Depression from Me

Dear Depression,

My dear friend, you have been that one constant relationship in my life that stuck with me through thick and thin. What a long and complicated relationship we have had. Not once did you leave my side regardless of how low the lows got or how high the highs would get. Not once did you leave my side for many, many years! You have been like an old, reliable friend who, at times, would claim to know what was best for me. Such dedication on your part made you an unwelcome yet a beloved aspect of myself. You were there for me in ways that I could not be…because of you.

Depression, my dear friend, you taught me that there is self-healing, something to learn, and nuggets of wisdom to pass on to others in almost every aspect of our daily lives. I thank you for not giving up on me but for continuing to hone in on the parts of me that called in all the triggers, traumas, and individuals who entered my life for a reason or a season. You have taught me how to identify, how to acknowledge, and how to take accountability for anything and everything that I, and only I, am responsible for in my life.

It took quite a number of years for me to catch on to why you were so persistent in not leaving my side. It took longer than it should have for me to pay attention to the nudges in life that were trying to teach me a lesson or get my attention. They are there for a reason and are not meant to be ignored—and definitely not meant to be repressed or suppressed. I thank you for the lessons you have taught me.

As interesting, drama-filled, and consistently loyal as you have been, it is time that we go our separate ways. Yes, I'm breaking up with you. Your reasons for existing within me have been purged, and your hard work can cease. You can retire! That is my wish for you, my friend. I appreciate the lessons. Let me be clear...this is not "see you later." This is our final goodbye.

Take care,
Elba Raquel

Epilogue

During one pivotal moment in my transformation, I participated in a guided meditation with my mindset coach, Lisa J. As I closed my eyes and allowed myself to fully immerse in the experience, I was guided to imagine entering a room. What I saw in my mind's eye was expansive—a vast room with floor-to-ceiling windows showcasing a lush, vibrant landscape. I saw countless shades of green, rich and deeply pigmented, just like the ones I'd marveled at in Tokyo's shrines and city gardens.

Inside, I took a seat at a stunning wooden table with raw edges. Across from me was an empty chair. Suddenly, a little girl appeared. She had olive skin, brown hair, and warm brown eyes. It was me—the little girl who once walked down the hallway in her shiny, black Mary Janes. Her smile was radiant, pure, and full of joy. In that moment, I felt an overwhelming surge of love, care, and pride from my inner child. I could feel my energy shifting from within—my inner *fuego* intensifying. As I poured love into healing my inner child, something profound began to happen. My energy lightened, and I could actually feel the change taking place. It brought me to tears then, and even now, as I write this, I'm filled with emotion.

Epilogue

Self-love is truly the most beautiful, rewarding, and fulfilling kind of love there is. It's pure and unconditional. Don't you want to give yourself that gift?

The little me sat in the chair across from me, and we held hands, talking for what felt like ages. The messages I received during that meditation are for me to hold close, but let me tell you—since that day, I have not been the same. I now give myself more space, more grace, and so much more love. This healing journey has brought me back to my true self, to my authenticity, more than any other process I have undergone. I am healing, and I feel like a new person, energetically. Something deep inside has shifted back into place. I acknowledge the progress I continue to make, and I'm deeply grateful for that experience. It's been instrumental in my success with my Emotional Intelligence Formula.

My friend, I live my life without regrets. I appreciate the good, the bad, and the ugly because it has all shaped me into the person I am today. Those difficult moments birthed my EIF. Trying to manage stress, depression, and anxiety during those times led to the natural development of this formula. It's been tested over and over, and each time it has guided me through my lowest points, equipping me with the mindset, strength, courage, and love needed to rise up and embrace life's highs.

I'm living proof that it works.

Today, I can confidently say that my fire—my *fuego*—is back. I am deeply in love with my life, and more importantly, I am in love with myself just as I am. And as I continue to evolve into an even better version of myself, that love will only grow. A few years ago, I didn't even like myself—let alone love myself—and for many years before that, I didn't either. This transformation is nothing short of radical.

I'll always be a work in progress, and I'm completely at peace with that. There's a sense of joy and serenity in my life now that is unshakable, and it forms the very core of my existence.

I've learned that I am in control of my mental health, my emotional intelligence, my thoughts, my relationships, my joy, and my peace. I get to choose who shares my time, space, and energy. I no longer entertain relationships that don't expand my life or consciousness. I am fully in control of my life—no one else. And that, my friend, is both liberating and priceless. It's beautiful. It's peaceful. It's joyful. It's exactly what I want it to be. It's the *fuego* within me!

Not only am I unrecognizable—so is my life.

The most miraculous thing of all is that once I shifted my mindset, everything else followed. I started meeting more like-minded people, especially women who have become my closest friends and strongest supporters. They're so invested in my dream that they've even contributed great ideas for my book (thank you, my dear friends—you know who you are!). And that, in itself, makes all the self-improvement worth it! Wouldn't that be worth it for you?

When you make those mindset changes and commit to practicing them, your *fuego* will start to shine from within. It'll transform your outer world in ways you never imagined.

As you work hard, you'll start attracting everything you've been striving for. And you might even get what I call a "something better." Yes, you read that right! You could receive exactly what you want from life… or something even better!

Believe me, my friend, it can be your new reality too!

My Notes

My Notes

My Notes

My Notes

www.ingramcontent.com/pod-product-compliance
Lightning Source LLC
LaVergne TN
LVHW021810070526
838027LV00050B/214/J